Major papers and projects		Tests and quizzes	
Title	Date due*	Subject of test	Date

* Start major projects at least one month before they are due.

COLLEGE STUDY SKILLS

COLLEGE STUDY SKILLS

James F. Shepherd

Queensborough Community College,
The City University of New York

HOUGHTON MIFFLIN COMPANY   Boston
Dallas   Geneva, Illinois   Hopewell, New Jersey
Palo Alto   London

Printed in the U.S.A.

Library of Congress Catalog Card Number: 78-69553

ISBN: 0-395-26261-5

This book is dedicated to the memory of my mother,
Lyndal Roosevelt Shepherd, and to Margot Walthers
and Josephine P. Ives.

Contents

Preface

Those of us who teach reading in colleges are confronted with the conflict that if we spend most of our time helping students improve their reading skills, we have little time to teach them the study skills they need to survive in college. *College Study Skills* was written to help resolve this conflict. Using the theory and practice of improving reading comprehension, this book provides a complete course in study and test-taking skills for first-year college students. *College Study Skills* makes it possible to help students acquire the study skills they need to do college work while they also increase their ability to comprehend written material.

In addition, *College Study Skills* contains sufficient explanatory information and exercises to ensure that most students who understand the explanations and do the exercises will acquire the skills this book teaches. All explanations and practice materials are written in language that can be understood by today's average college freshmen. Exercises have been carefully developed so that there are the correct number of exercises of the right length to permit most students to achieve the objectives of instruction. Though users of this book may wish to use their favorite supplementary materials, they will be relieved of the constant search for additional materials for the practice and reinforcement of skills taught in the basic text.

The materials for exercises were selected as being appropriate for skills development, representative of materials students read in college, appropriate in reading difficulty, and interesting to students. Also, since most exercises contain information that is new to many first-year students, the exercises broaden students' knowledge and provide bases for worthwhile discussions.

The text is arranged in the sequence that I have found most practical for providing skills development to students who are concurrently enrolled in other college courses, but other sequences are equally logical and may be more suitable in certain instances. For example, if students are not taking other college courses at the time they study this book, it is often desirable to teach basic organizational skills (Lessons 14–22) before teaching other lessons. It is also practical to teach the lessons for test-taking skills (Lessons 23–30) concurrently with the lessons for organizational skills (Lessons 14–22) or the lessons for basic study procedures (Lessons 7–13). This book was written to make a variety of teaching sequences possible.

While I assume responsibility for the contents of *College Study Skills,* I am indebted to the hundreds of students at Queensborough Community College who took an active interest in its development. Also, while the text was in manuscript form, suggestions for improvements were made by the following reviewers: Helen Gilbart, St. Petersburg Junior College; Madeline S. Nixon, St. Petersburg Junior College; William S. Tharp, Schenectady

County Community College; Edward F. Wightman, Hudson Valley Community College; and Joseph Zielinski, Tarrant County Junior College. I benefited greatly from their suggestions and hope they will be gratified to find some of their thoughts reflected in the final work.

Special appreciation is extended to my good friends Professors Joseph Hosey and Harriet Krantz for reading the manuscript before I sent it to Houghton Mifflin Company. The encouragement of these talented teachers and the generosity with which they have shared their expertise with me are among the many reasons Queensborough Community College has been a happy academic home for nine years.

Professor Emeritus Josephine Ives of New York University also read the manuscript and, in her typically thorough manner, made many important contributions to the final form of the text you now see. I am indebted to her for this, but much more for her many contributions to my professional development over the years, for her intellectual honesty, and for her friendship.

J. F. S.

To the Student

I know you are unique, different from any other person who ever lived. But, for a moment, I would like to imagine that you are similar to some of the hundreds of students who took a part in helping decide which lessons and which exercises should be included in *College Study Skills*.

They were people full of hope that college would help them achieve their worthwhile goals in life, but sometimes they were fearful that they might not succeed in college. They were people who wanted assistance in reaching their goals, but sometimes they were uncertain whether anybody could give them the kind of help they wanted. Many of them are college graduates today, others went to work or married without finishing college, others are still pursuing a college degree. But together we all learned and grew as they told me what they wanted to learn and helped me improve the lessons you will study in this book.

One of the difficulties I had in writing this book was that sometimes students did not know during the first weeks of college exactly which skills they were going to need. For example, when I taught outlining skills, some students complained they did not need to know how to outline. But then, later in the school year, the same students often thanked me for teaching them to outline; they discovered later it was a skill they needed. This book contains *only* those skills that students found most useful in helping them do their best in college.

This is why I would like very much to imagine that you are similar to some of the students who helped in the development of this book. I would like to think that the skills that helped them become better students are the same ones that will help you have a happier college experience.

WILL YOU SUCCEED IN COLLEGE?

If you are similar to some of the students I have known, you are at least a little concerned whether you will do well in college. Many students have the ability to do well in college but do not do well because they really do not want to be in school and do not have the desire to do well. Unless you have a good reason for being in school, it may be difficult for you to accept all the demands college will place on you. Some people go to college simply because there is nothing else to do or because most of the people they know are going. These are not adequate reasons to go through all the aggravations necessary to earn a college degree.

Usually those who do well in college are there because they are preparing themselves for a specific occupation or because they want some other benefit that college can bring. They have a clear, worthwhile reason for wanting to get the most out of their college experience. Having a good reason for being in school motivates them to do the very best they can and helps them to endure difficulties they encounter. They are concerned about doing well, but they do not question their ability to succeed. They know that the people who graduate from colleges are people very much like themselves and that a college degree is within their reach.

If you have not already done so, you should give yourself a good reason for being in college because it will make your college years more meaningful to you. If you have difficulty determining why you are in school, turn to the friend, relative, teacher, or counselor who helps you when you need to make decisions. You will deal effectively with difficult problems related to your college life if you know why you are in school and are determined to succeed.

CAN YOU BECOME A BETTER STUDENT?

Many of the students I have known managed to do well in high school without having developed the study skills that are necessary for college. They would have failed or done very poorly in college if they had not learned the kinds of skills taught in this book.

If you have decided you really want to be in college, if you are determined to succeed in college, and if you are interested in knowing how you can achieve this goal, the things you learn in *College Study Skills* can help you become a better student. You will learn the most efficient way to approach reading assignments, how to mark your textbooks, how to make notes for studying, and how to do your best when you take tests. You will follow very specific instructions for solving various kinds of study problems. The reason for this is *not* to encourage you to follow those instructions slavishly every time you study, but

1. to open your mind to possibilities for studying that you may not have thought about or may not discover easily on your own, and
2. to provide a basis for discussing study procedures and the solutions to study problems.

In order to learn the skills needed for learning how to learn, you need specific and clear procedures to follow. However, when you study on your own, you do not have to study in *exactly* the way you were taught to study, any more than when you drive a car, you have to drive it in exactly the way you were taught to drive. You learn about driving by driving, and you will learn about studying by studying. *The purpose of this book is to provide you with information and experiences you can use to develop your own distinctive procedures for studying, but you cannot develop good study habits unless you practice them when studying for your college courses.*

You should not expect to become an expert student by studying this book or practicing for one semester what you learn here. Study is a complex procedure, and to become an expert at something complex takes more than three or four months. The things you learn in this book will give you a foundation for studying that you can build on throughout your college career and throughout your lifetime.

If you are not similar to students that I have known, you will be after you have read this book and solved the problems in it. At that time you will have shared with me and them experiences that helped us become better students and made us, in this way, a little more alike.

J. F. S.

COLLEGE STUDY SKILLS

Part I. Introduction to Study Skills

The primary purposes of this book are to teach you ways to make the best use of your study time and to give you information that you can use to do your best in college. In the first part of the book, you are asked to take a look at yourself as a student and also at your college and its academic system. Then you are introduced to a process that you may feel you already know quite well—the process known as *study*.

The lessons in Part 1 are divided into the two groups shown at the left.

Part 1: Introduction to Study Skills

© 1979 by Houghton Mifflin Company

Lesson I. The Serious Student

People who do well in college take being in college seriously. They treat college as one of the most important experiences in their lives. They give their college study all the attention that they would give to doing good work on a job they do not want to lose. They believe that college will help them live a better life, and they put everything they have into doing their best in their studies.

These people know that the record they accumulate in college is something that can never be taken away from them—it is theirs forever. They know that this record will help them get into other schools or get a job they want, so they do everything they can to make certain their college record is as good as it can be.

1. They practically never miss a class.
2. They know exactly what to do if they must be absent from a class.
3. They almost always turn in assignments on time.
4. They are in class the day a test or quiz is given.
5. They schedule their study time.

When students fail to do even *one* of these things, their college experience is much less happy than it could be. When students are absent from class, do not turn in assignments on time, or are absent the day of a test, college professors are likely to become seriously concerned. Most students who do even one of these things end up doing poorly in a course. Students who follow this pattern of behavior in many courses usually end up dropping out of college.

The next pages explain the importance of each of the characteristics of serious students. Even if you already understand their importance, you will probably find in the explanations several suggestions you can use.

GO TO ALL CLASSES

Some schools have no official attendance requirements for passing courses, but most colleges expect their students to attend *all* class sessions. Also, colleges usually do not distinguish between "excused" and "unexcused" absences as some high schools do. College professors expect students to be serious about learning and rightfully assume that they will be in class unless there is an excellent reason for their not being there.

The purposes of most class sessions in college are to help students understand the course materials and to give them information and experiences they will not find in reading on their own. It is unusual if students who miss these offerings do as well as students who take advantage of them by going to class. When instructors tell you they want you to come to classes, they are telling you they are interested in you and want to teach you what they know. These people deserve your respect, because they want to help you have a successful college career.

Since you are generally expected to attend classes, don't ask a teacher, "How many absences am I allowed in this course?" Instead, be serious about your schooling by going to all your classes and profiting from them as much as you can. Not attending classes regularly in a course may be an indication that you should not be taking the course or that you do not really want to be in college. You should discuss this problem with somebody who can help you make a decision. Since few students can do well in college courses when they miss many class sessions, students who cut classes should decide to start attending them or to withdraw from them.

On the inside front cover of this book is a chart for keeping a record of your absences from the courses you are taking this term. If you miss more than one out of ten classes in a course, you have definitely missed too many classes.

ASSUME RESPONSIBILITY FOR ABSENCES

No matter how hard you try to attend every class, it is likely that you will miss a class from time to time. You may be absent on the day an instructor announces a quiz or gives an assignment for the next session, and you will very likely miss a lecture on which you will need notes. Your instructors are not going to telephone you to tell you about a quiz or assignment, nor are they likely to repeat lectures for you.

After students have been absent, they sometimes ask their instructors, "Did I miss anything important?" Try to avoid asking this question of your professors. First, it implies that what typically goes on in class is not important. Second, it suggests that your professors should tell you all the important things you might have missed. This practice is annoying to teachers, because the day you were absent other students were probably also absent and your instructors do not have time to give individualized instruction to all students who have missed a class.

Instructors also do not like to hear students say "I didn't know about the quiz because I was absent the day you announced it." This statement is annoying because from an instructor's point of view it is the responsibility of serious students to know everything that happens in class sessions—even when they are absent.

How is it possible to get lecture notes you missed or to find out if a quiz or assignment was announced on a day you were absent? Simple! Exchange names with somebody in each of your classes and give them a call if you are absent. An easy way to get a copy of missed lecture notes is to photocopy the notes of a classmate in your college library.

On the inside front cover of this book is a chart for recording the names and telephone numbers of people in each of your classes whom you can contact for lecture notes and assignments if you should miss a class. Choose good students who attend class regularly.

TURN IN ASSIGNMENTS ON TIME

When a teacher announces that an assignment is due on a certain day, the teacher expects to receive the assignment on that day and not on some other day. A teacher cannot help being concerned for the student who fails to turn in an assignment on the day it is due. Instructors know from experience that students who do not turn in assignments on time are all too frequently the same ones who do poorly on tests, receive low final grades, or fail courses.

The major reason that students fail to complete assignments on time is that they underestimate how long it will take to write a term paper or to do all the work necessary for a major term project. Some study skills books advise students to begin writing term papers the day they are assigned. This is good advice, but practically nobody follows it. However, you will probably run into serious difficulty if you do not begin working on major projects *at least* three or four weeks before they are due.

No matter how hard you try, it is likely that sometime in your college career you will be unable to complete a project on time. If you know that this is going to happen, go to your teacher *at least* one week before the project is due and explain your problem. Set a specific date when the late assignment will be delivered, and then be certain to turn it in on the date you have set. This action will demonstrate to your instructor that you are serious about your studies and is likely to make a favorable impression.

On the inside front cover of this book is a chart on which to record the term papers and major projects you must do this term. Write the dates these assignments are due, and refer to them often to make certain you are allowing enough time to complete the papers or projects before they are due.

GO TO ALL TESTS

It is a good idea to prepare well for tests and to go to class the day a test is given. Usually teachers rely heavily on quiz and test scores to help them determine final course grades. The assigning of final grades is a very difficult job, and it becomes even more difficult when quiz or test scores are missing for students.

It is not possible to state how most instructors handle the problem of missing test scores, but it is known that if no make-up test is taken, frequently a missed test is automatically given a failing grade. The failing grade is then often averaged in with the student's other grades to determine the final grade. As a result, when average or better-than-average students miss tests and fail to make them up, they usually receive a lower final grade than they would have received if they had taken all the tests.

Try to make particular effort to be present the day an instructor gives his or her *first* test in a course. When students take an instructor's first test, they learn, among other things, the instructor's style of testing and the type of information that the instructor considers to be important. This knowledge is very helpful to students in studying for all the other tests an instructor gives.

Finally, keep in mind that you are given an advantage by a teacher who gives several tests during a term. If an instructor gives many tests, you may do poorly on one or two but still receive a satisfactory final course grade. However, if a teacher gives only a few tests, you will probably have to do well on all of them to receive a satisfactory final grade.

On the inside front cover of this book is a chart on which to record the dates of tests and quizzes that will be given in your courses this term. Keep an accurate record and refer to it often so you can allow plenty of time to study before the day of the test.

**SCHEDULE YOUR
STUDY TIME**

The rule of thumb for estimating study time for college courses is two hours of study for each hour of class. In other words, the student with fifteen hours of classes a week should plan for thirty hours of study outside of class!

Studies have found that most students do not spend this much time studying for all their courses. If you are not doing as well as you believe you should be doing in college, you should map out your week in a schedule to see if you are allowing two hours of study for each hour of class. If you are not, you should schedule more study time.

There are several things to keep in mind when you set up your study schedule.

1. Do not use your experiences in high school as a guide to how much study time you should allow. If you want to do as well in college as you did in high school, you will need to allow *more* time for studying; if you want to do better, you will need to allow *much more* time for studying.
2. Most school terms have a "snowball" effect in which work tends to accumulate during the last half or last third of a term. You should keep this in mind and schedule time to complete term papers and projects as early in the term as possible. If you do not, you will find yourself writing term papers at the time you should be preparing for final examinations.
3. Make a realistic schedule that allows time for meals, visits with friends, and your favorite forms of amusement. If you do not include the pleasures of life in your schedule, you will not follow it. Do not make a schedule you are not going to follow.
4. Your schedule will need to be revised from time to time as the requirements for some courses increase and the requirements for others decrease.

On the inside back cover of this book is a chart you can use to set up your study schedule. Write your study schedule in pencil so you can change it when revisions are necessary.

**PRACTICE BEING
A SERIOUS STUDENT**

On the inside front cover of this book there is a chart you can use to keep records of absences, names of people in your courses, dates on which major assignments are due, and dates of tests. On the inside back cover there is a chart for making a schedule of your classes and study time. *Fill in these charts with the information that belongs in them.*

If at any time during your college career you find you are not doing as well as you should be doing, please reread this lesson. Many students do not do their best in college simply because they have not developed the basic habits that are characteristic of serious students.

Lesson 2. Your College's Rules and Regulations

Most colleges publish a paperback book known as the *bulletin* or *catalog*. This book contains a description of the rules and regulations for students in the school. Although most college catalogs are as difficult to understand as an insurance contract, they contain much information that is of importance to people who are interested in earning a college degree.

Many students receive lower grades in college than they should because they make mistakes that could have been avoided if they had taken the time to read and understand their college catalog. Your college expects you to know the information printed in its catalog, and this lesson will help you learn some of that information so you may avoid making a mistake you might later regret.

The answers to the following questions will give you a better understanding of how college is different from other schools you have attended. *If* the answer to a question appears in your college catalog, that answer is the one to use as the response to a question. The best way to do this lesson is to discuss the questions in class, referring to your instructor and the glossary (page 269) for the correct answers as necessary. Eliminate questions that do not pertain to your college.

1. Give the meanings of the following terms:

a. *Grade point average*

_____

_____

_____

b. *Curriculum for a degree*

_____

_____

_____

c. *Prerequisite* for a course

_____

_____

_____

d. *Probation*

_____

_____

_____

e. *Matriculated student*

_____

_____

_____

f. *Transcript*

_____

_____

_____

g. *Audit* a course

_____

_____

_____

2. What are the steps or procedures one must follow to change curriculums at your college?

_____

_____

_____

_____

3. According to the official attendance requirements of your college, what is the maximum number of absences allowed for a course that meets

a. two times a week? _____

b. three times a week? _____

c. four times a week? _____

If no attendance requirements are stated in your college bulletin, assume that no more than a 15-percent absence rate is allowed.

4. What is the maximum number of credits a matriculated student at your college may carry without receiving special permission?

_____

5. What is the maximum number of hours a matriculated student at your college may carry without receiving special permission?

_____

6. What is the minimum number of credits a student at your college must carry to be considered a full-time student?

_____

7. What is the minimum number of hours a student at your college must carry to be considered a full-time student?

_____

8. According to your college catalog, what is the meaning of each of these letter grades?

A means _____

B means _____

C means _____

D means _____

F means _____

9. What letter grades are used by your college to compute grade point averages?

_____

_____

10. What W grades are given at your college, and what is the meaning and importance of each of them?

_____

_____

_____

_____

_____

_____

11. What is the meaning and importance of the INC (incomplete) grade?

_____

_____

_____

_____

_____

12. If students receive a grade of F in a course that is required in their degree program,

    a. will they need to repeat the course? _____

    b. will the F lower their grade point average? _____

13. What is the minimum grade point average that students at your college must have in order to be in good standing after completing

    a. 12 credits? _____

    b. 24 credits? _____

    c. 36 credits? _____

14. What is the minimum grade point average that students must have in order to graduate from your college?

_____

15. If students are put on probation (lose matriculated status) due to low grades, how much time are they given to raise their grades?

_____

Lesson 3. The Grading System

**NUMBER GRADES AND
LETTER GRADES**

Instructors usually evaluate students' work with number grades or letter grades. Many times students who are familiar with number grades are not certain how to interpret letter grades and students who are familiar with letter grades are not certain how to interpret number grades.

Most colleges and universities agree that specific letter grades are equivalent to specific number grades. Table 3.1 shows these generally agreed upon correspondences. Study your college catalog and make changes in Table 3.1 if your school uses a different system. Notice that there are no A+, F+, or F− grades and that number grades for A and A− letter grades are divided differently than number grades for other letter grades.

Some instructors tell students that number grades for certain tests have different letter grade values than those shown in Table 3.1. However, if your instructors do *not* state the letter grade equivalents for the number grades they give, you have every reason to believe that the equivalents are the same as those shown in the table.

Study Table 3.1 and then write the letter grades for the number grades that are given in the chart labeled Table 3.2, using pluses and minuses where necessary. After you have done the first column, check your answers and then move on to the second column.

Table 3.1   Correspondence Between Letter Grades and Number Grades

Letter grade	Number grade		
	With a minus	With no plus or minus	With a plus
A	90–95	96–100	—
B	80–83	84–86	87–89
C	70–73	74–76	77–79
D	60–63	64–66	67–69
F	—	0–59	—

**THE GRADE POINT
AVERAGE**

The *grade point average* is a number that identifies the average grade that students have received for the courses they have taken. This number is important to students because schools use it to compare people and to decide who should be admitted to or kept in schools, and employers may use it to determine who should be hired to fill job openings.

Table 3.2

Number grade	Letter grade		Number grade	Letter grade
1. 91	_____		1. 87	_____
2. 72	_____		2. 75	_____
3. 81	_____		3. 73	_____
4. 96	_____		4. 81	_____
5. 79	_____		5. 98	_____
6. 85	_____		6. 86	_____
7. 64	_____		7. 63	_____
8. 76	_____		8. 64	_____
9. 77	_____		9. 76	_____
10. 68	_____		10. 78	_____
11. 83	_____		11. 60	_____
12. 66	_____		12. 59	_____
13. 89	_____		13. 69	_____
14. 74	_____		14. 70	_____
15. 58	_____		15. 89	_____
16. 61	_____		16. 90	_____
17. 84	_____		17. 65	_____
18. 59	_____		18. 80	_____

Changing Letter Grades to Number Values. The grade point average is used when students receive letter grades for courses they take. To find the average letter grade, the letter grades are first changed into number values. The numbers that most colleges assign to letter grades, whether or not they have a plus or minus, are as follows:

```
A    4.00
B    3.00
C    2.00
D    1.00
F    0.00  _____ *
```

Some colleges give .30 more value for plus grades and .30 less value for minus grades. When this system is used, D+ has a value of 1.30, C− has a value of 1.70, C+ has a value of 2.30, and so on. Other colleges give .35 more value for plus grades and .35 less value for minus grades. When this is the case, D+ has a value of 1.35, C− has a value of 1.65, C+ has a value of 2.35, and so on. Learn the system used by your school so you can understand better how your grade point average is computed and thus interpret your transcripts correctly.

Beside the first column of letter grades in Table 3.3, write the number value your college gives for each letter grade. After you have done the first column, check your answers (refer to your college catalog if necessary) and then complete the second column.

Table 3.3

1. A	_____		1. C	_____
2. C−	_____		2. B−	_____
3. B+	_____		3. F	_____
4. D−	_____		4. D	_____
5. B	_____		5. C+	_____
6. D+	_____		6. A−	_____
7. A−	_____		7. A	_____
8. C+	_____		8. D+	_____
9. D	_____		9. C−	_____
10. F	_____		10. B	_____
11. B−	_____		11. B+	_____
12. C	_____		12. D−	_____

* If your college assigns a value of 0.00 to grades other than F, write those grades on this line.

Computing the Grade Point Average. A *grade point average* is found by dividing the *total grade points* of a student by the *total credits*. The following sample problem shows how total grade points and total credits may be found for a student who received B's and C's in four three-credit courses.

Letter grade	Grade point value		Credits		Grade points
B	3	×	3	=	9
B	3	×	3	=	9
C	2	×	3	=	6
C	2	×	3	=	6
			12		30

This student has a total of 30 grade points and a total of 12 credits. Study the problem to understand how these values were determined. The student's grade point average may be found by dividing 30 (total grade points) by 12 (total credits), which gives a result of 2.50, the student's grade point average.

When students have accumulated many credits, it is easier to find a grade point average by grouping all the credits for each letter grade. The preceding problem could have been solved by grouping credits of B and credits of C together, as follows:

Letter grade	Grade point value		Credits		Grade points
B	3	×	6	=	18
C	2	×	6	=	12
			12		30

When the problem is arranged in this way, the student still has 30 total grade points and 12 total credits, and the grade point average is still 2.50.

PRACTICE WITH THE GRADE POINT AVERAGE

The problems for this lesson will be solved using the short-cut method for computation, and only the following grade point values will be used: 4.00, 3.00, 2.00, 1.00, and 0.00.

Class Practice

Grade Point Average

1. This problem is complete except for addition and division. Find the total grade points, total credits, and grade point average.

Letter grade	Grade point value		Credits		Grade points
A	4	×	2	=	8
B	3	×	3	=	9
C	2	×	6	=	12
D	1	×	4	=	4

Grade point average = _____

2. In this problem you are given only the number of credits a student has for certain letter grades. You must enter the grade point values for the letter grades. Do the multiplication, addition, and division to find the grade point average.

Letter grade	Grade point value		Credits		Grade points
A		×	4	=	
B		×	4	=	
C		×	6	=	
D		×	6	=	__

Grade point average = _____

3. Do this problem in the same way you did Problem 2. Pay special attention to the F grade.

Letter grade	Grade point value		Credits		Grade points
C		×	6	=	
D		×	3	=	
F		×	6	=	__

Grade point average = _____

4. This problem is the same as Problem 3 except that the student officially withdrew from 6 credits.

Letter grade	Grade point value		Credits		Grade points
C		×	6	=	
D		×	3	=	
W		×	<u>6</u>	=	__

Grade point average = _____

Assignment 1

Grade Point Average

Find the grade point average for each of the following problems.

1.

Letter grade	Grade point value		Credits		Grade points
A		×	3	=	
B		×	3	=	
C		×	<u>9</u>	=	__

Grade point average = _____

2.

Letter grade	Grade point value		Credits		Grade points
B		×	2	=	
C		×	8	=	
D		×	<u>5</u>	=	__

Grade point average = _____

3.

Letter grade	Grade point value		Credits		Grade points
C		×	6	=	
D		×	6	=	
F		×	<u>3</u>	=	__

Grade point average = _____

4.

Letter grade	Grade point value		Credits		Grade points
C		×	6	=	
D		×	6	=	
W		×	<u>3</u>	=	__

Grade point average = _____

Assignment 2

Grade Point Average

Find the grade point average for each of the following problems.

1.

Letter grade	Grade point value		Credits		Grade points
A		×	12	=	
B		×	8	=	
C		×	<u>15</u>	=	__

Grade point average = _____

2.

Letter grade	Grade point value		Credits		Grade points
B		×	10	=	
C		×	6	=	
D		×	<u>2</u>	=	__

Grade point average = _____

3.

Letter grade	Grade point value		Credits		Grade points
B		×	6	=	
C		×	6	=	
D		×	6	=	
F		×	<u>12</u>	=	__

Grade point average = _____

4.

Letter grade	Grade point value		Credits		Grade points
B		×	6	=	
C		×	6	=	
D		×	6	=	
W		×	<u>12</u>	=	__

Grade point average = _____

Lesson 4. Taking Lecture Notes

Most college professors expect students to keep a record of what is said in class, and they use the information covered in lectures as the basis for writing test questions. Therefore, unless students have good lecture notes, they are not able to prepare properly for tests. This lesson is placed at the beginning of the book to introduce you to the basic things you should know about taking lecture notes. Other lessons in this book will teach you additional skills you can use to improve your ability to take useful lecture notes.

**CHARACTERISTICS OF
GOOD LECTURE NOTES**

In Figure 4.1 you will find an example of lecture notes taken in the traditional format. Other note-taking methods are very similar to the one used in preparing these sample lecture notes.

Notice how well-organized the notes in Figure 4.1 are: (1) the name of the course, the professor, the date, and the topic of the lecture are in the heading, (2) the major points stand out clearly, and (3) the details are listed under the major points in an orderly fashion.

The sample notes are a rephrased summary of the things the lecturer said. Good note-takers do not try to write down a speaker's words exactly, but rather translate the speaker's words into their own words. When people change a speaker's words into words of their own, they are engaging in a complex and creative activity that shows that they understand the ideas the speaker is communicating.

A final characteristic of good lecture notes is that they contain important words, numbers, and things drawn on the chalkboard by a lecturer. Often professors write a word on the board because they intend to ask a test question about it. Such items should be marked for special attention. Also, professors usually do not draw diagrams, tables, or illustrations on the board unless the information is particularly important for students to record and remember.

**FINDING MAJOR POINTS
IN LECTURES**

It is more difficult to identify the major points in lectures than in material from printed pages because ideas are usually much better organized and worked out when they are written down than when they are presented in speech. Also, written material is presented under various kinds of headings that help us understand the major points that are being made. These kinds of organizational aids are not available in speech. Lecturers do, however, have four basic techniques that help students find the main things they say: (1) they pause, (2) they use repetition, (3) they use introductory phrases, and (4) they write on the chalkboard.

Figure 4.1   An Example of Well-organized Lecture Notes Made in the Traditional Format

Sociology 101, 11/7/83   O'Sullivan, Topic: "Deviance"

Who commits most crimes?
   1. Adolescents and young adults
   2. Mostly males (6 to 1)
   3. People in cities (5 to 1)
   4. People with low education, low income, and low-class occupations

Drug use
   1. About 200,000 heroin users in U.S.A. — tend to be young, male, living in cities
   2. Marijuana use is increasing
      — 42% of college students have used it (1971 poll)
      — 11% of adults have used it (1972 poll, up from 4% in 1969)

Alcoholism
   1. 6% to 10% of adults in U.S.A. are alcoholics — 2/3 of adults drink
   2. Alcoholics tend to be lower class, Catholic, mid-forties, live in large cities of Northeast or West

Suicide
   1. About 20,000 do it each year
   2. 7 out of 10 are men
   3. Tend to be 60's or older
   4. Whites, mostly
   5. Unmarried
   6. Protestants
   7. Upper and lower class (not middle class)

© 1979 by Houghton Mifflin Company

Pause. In speech the pause is one of the most effective forms of emphasis. If you listen carefully, you will find that a good lecturer makes a slight pause just before saying something that is important for you to record in your notes as a major point.

Repetition. Repetition is the second method used by lecturers to indicate that a statement is important. When a lecturer repeats the same statement one or more times, experienced students know that the statement belongs in notes. Often, repetition and pause are used together; a lecturer might pause before making an important statement, pause a second time, and then repeat the statement.

Introductory Phrases. The third clue to the organization of a lecture is the use of introductory phrases such as "the four points to consider are" or "the six main parts are." Such statements are your clue to exactly how many items should be included in a list of details.

The Chalkboard. Putting information on the chalkboard is the fourth important method instructors use that helps students take good notes. Whenever a professor writes a word or draws a diagram on the board, it should be placed in lecture notes and marked for special attention when reviewing for a test. Words written on the chalkboard are likely to be either those that are difficult to spell or those that are most important to learn about.

LISTENING FOR WORDS THAT SIGNAL IMPORTANCE

The introductory phrases lecturers use that help students organize their notes often include a word that signals importance. Experienced students are aware of these words and often underline them for emphasis:

> There are three <u>characteristics of</u> the amoeba that distinguish it from other protozoa.
> For purposes of analysis, there are five <u>steps</u> in the selling process.
> There are two <u>benefits of</u> the defense mechanism of substitution.

The following list includes some of these *signal words* you should listen for in lectures and mark for special attention when you study:

importance of	summary	comparison between
advantages of	conclusion	parts of
benefits of	description of	history of
disadvantages of	types of	uses of
problems of	kinds of	purposes of
causes of	characteristics of	functions of
results of	differences between	steps of
effects of	contrast between	methods of
evaluation of	similarities between	how to
criticism of		

**REVIEWING YOUR
LECTURE NOTES**

It is possible that you will take lecture notes in September and not be tested on them until November. If you do not understand your lecture notes in September, you will certainly not understand them three months later. Thus, it is very important to review your notes as soon as possible after a lecture session to make certain that you understand thoroughly what you wrote down and that your notes are complete. If anything about your notes is unclear or incomplete, you should look in your textbook, consult with another student, or ask questions of your professor to clarify or complete your notes while they are still fresh in your mind.

**ASKING QUESTIONS
OF PROFESSORS**

Some students dominate classes by constantly asking questions, but most students do not ask their professors the questions that would really help them learn. When you review your lecture notes, make a list of the questions you have and ask them in the next class session. Experienced teachers know that if one student is confused about a point of information, other students are also likely to be confused. Your well-considered questions not only will help you, but also will help your instructor eliminate the confusion that might be in other students' minds.

If for any reason you do not want to ask questions during classes, go to your professors before or after class to get the answers to your questions. You will find that most college teachers are interested in having students learn their subject matter and that most of them will be pleased to give you the answers to your questions or to help you find the answers.

STUDYING LECTURE NOTES

Specific suggestions for studying lecture notes in preparation for a test are given in Lesson 13.

**READING THE TEXT
AND LECTURE NOTES**

Sometimes professors lecture in such a way that students must read the textbook before class in order to understand the content of the lectures. In other instances they lecture with the intention that what they say will make it easier for students to understand what they will read in the textbook. Therefore, study your textbooks in relation to the lectures and then decide which method is appropriate for each course. If you have difficulty understanding a professor's lectures, this may be an indication that you should read the text *before* you go to class.

**ADAPTING TO DIFFERENT
LECTURING STYLES**

Some doctors have an excellent way of explaining illnesses to their patients, and others do not. Similarly, some lecturers have an excellent way of making course content understandable to students, while others do not. Most college professors have not spent much time in the formal study of public speaking; they have developed their lecturing styles by observing other teachers and from their own classroom experiences.

Since training for lecturing is so varied, you should consider yourself fortunate when you have instructors who make their course content understandable and interesting. Do not expect each of your professors to be an expert in communicating ideas. In some courses you will feel that your professors give you very little help in learning the things you need to learn. When this happens, it is especially important for you to have acquired the other study skills that are explained in this book, so that you will be able to learn efficiently even when instructors provide little assistance.

GETTING LECTURE NOTES WHEN YOU MISS CLASS

In Lesson 1 it was suggested that if you are absent the day lectures are given, you should get copies of lecture notes from students in your classes. It was also advised that an easy way to copy notes is to use a photocopying machine in your school library.

However, *the notes you copy from a fellow student will seldom be as useful to you as your own notes when you study for tests*. Lecture notes are highly personal documents; the notes you make for a lecture will be different in many ways from the notes made by other students for the same lecture. You will make notes in a way that is meaningful to you, and other students will make notes in ways that make sense to them. Many difficulties are involved in trying to study from other students' notes; this is one reason it is very important for you to go to all your classes.

SELECTING A NOTEBOOK FOR LECTURE NOTES

At the beginning of school terms, most college bookstores put out great stacks of spiral notebooks, most of which measure 8½ by 11 inches. Other sizes and types of notebooks are sold in smaller quantities, because the 8½ by 11 inch spiral notebook is the type preferred by most experienced college students. If you have no good reason for doing otherwise, it is suggested that you purchase this size of notebook for keeping your lecture notes.

Spiral notebooks do, though, have some limitations of which you should be aware. First, if you are absent from class, it is not possible to integrate a copy of lecture notes into a spiral notebook. You will need to leave blank pages and copy notes into your spiral notebook. Also, some instructors return papers you will need to review before taking tests. If you take notes in a spiral notebook, you will need a three-ring binder in which to keep such papers. Important papers crammed haphazardly into a spiral notebook have a mysterious way of disappearing at the very moment they are needed.

GETTING PRACTICE TAKING LECTURE NOTES

There are three basic ways you may practice taking lecture notes:

1. by taking notes in any class
2. by taking notes in your study skills class
3. by taking notes from recorded lectures in your study skills class, reading laboratory, or learning center

The last two types of practice are extremely helpful for developing note-taking skills because after notes have been taken, they may be compared to a model and evaluated. If you compare your lecture notes to a model of lecture notes, you will gain confidence that you take good notes or you will discover what you must do to improve your note-taking abilities.

Lesson 5. Problems in Studying

This lesson provides some solutions to seven problems students frequently have when studying. It is certain to contain some suggestions you can put to use starting today.

LEARNING TO CONCENTRATE

"How can I learn to concentrate when I read?" If you have asked yourself this question, you, like most people, have had the experience of reading a page or two only to realize that you did not remember a thing of what you read. What probably happened is that your mind drifted off to something that happened earlier in the day, something that was worrying you, or something you would rather have been doing. The steps for improving concentration are incredibly easy to describe, but some people find them somewhat more difficult to put into practice. They are as follows.

First, before you sit down to study, you must *make the conscious decision that you are going to study* and that you are not going to do something else. Each time you study, you must decide that you want to spend some time learning the things you need to learn rather than spend that same time listening to a record, watching television, talking to a friend, or doing any one of the dozens of other things you might also do with your time. Until you make this clear decision, you will resent the time you spend studying and you will not be able to concentrate on what you read.

Second, once you have decided you will study, you must *know what you will study and how long you will study*. Do not sit staring at a stack of books wondering where to begin. Rather, before you sit down to study, spend some time analyzing exactly which subjects should be given priority and decide how much time you can reasonably spend studying those subjects.

Priorities are determined in light of whatever current assignments, upcoming tests, or upcoming major assignments are due. Once you have decided what to study, be logical about deciding how much time you will spend studying it. Do not set aside four hours to study for a mathematics course if you know you have only four hours to study and other courses also need attention; do not set aside an hour to read a chapter that you know will take three hours to read. In other words, learn to estimate how much time you have in your schedule to devote to studying and how much time will be needed to do different types of assignments. Information about scheduling your study time appears in Lesson 1, and a method for estimating the amount of time you need for reading assignments is given in this lesson.

Finally, *practice concentrating*. If you have read a page or two and do not remember what you read, stop reading and do something else. Go talk to somebody, call a friend on the phone, turn on the television, do anything; but stop reading, because there is no point in reading when you can't remember what you read. When you are ready to return to reading, write

26

down on a piece of paper the time you start reading. Then read until you find you are no longer concentrating, and write that time on the same piece of paper to determine how long you were able to concentrate. At first you may find you lose concentration after only five or six minutes, but do not let this discourage you. Continue this procedure every time you read, trying each time to extend your concentration by a minute or two. This simple procedure is guaranteed to help you increase your concentration. Also, of course, most of the lessons in this book will help you improve your concentration by giving you specific, worthwhile things to do when you study.

PLANNING THE TIME NEEDED FOR READING

Some students plan too little study time simply because they cannot estimate how long it will take them to read a certain number of pages in a particular book. "How," they wonder, "can I estimate how long it will take me to read this chapter?" The problem is that some books have more words on a page than others and some books are more difficult to read than others. It may take twice as long for you to read ten pages of a psychology textbook as it would to read ten pages of a speech textbook.

Learn to estimate how much time you need for reading a particular book. First, write the time in pencil at the place where you begin reading. After you have finished reading a few pages, write the time again. Then, count the pages and the time it took to read them. Do this a few times in each book you are studying and you will soon be able to estimate very accurately how long it will take you to read ten, twenty-five, or fifty pages of any book you are studying.

Knowing your reading rate for a specific textbook has another advantage in addition to enabling you to estimate how long it will take you to do a reading assignment—it can help you to avoid wasting study time. If, while studying, you find that you have spent an hour reading what you should have read in a half an hour, you have proof that you have wasted some time. Either you should try to speed up or you should go to some other study task, because you should not spend any more time reading a passage than is necessary.

UNDERSTANDING THE DIFFERENCE BETWEEN READING AND STUDYING

"Why is it that even though I understand what I read in my books, I can't remember it for tests?" If you have asked yourself this question, you know that it is not enough simply to understand something in order to take a test on it. If you read this morning's newspaper, you would understand it, but you would not do very well on a test of what you had read. You would need to *study* the newspaper in order to do well on a difficult test of its contents.

Reading and studying are two different things. *Reading* is the process we use to understand ideas that are presented in writing, but *studying* is the process we use to remember and recall information that we read or hear. The lessons in this book will teach you how to retain what you read by giving you methods to organize the things you want to learn, by showing you how to anticipate test questions you might be asked on the things you study, and by providing you with a means you can use to place the things you want to learn in your memory for the purpose of taking tests.

GETTING STARTED STUDYING

"I have a hard time getting started studying. How can I break this habit?" Does this sound like you? If so, try beginning each study session by doing the most routine or easiest things you need to do. Gradually, your mind will become adjusted so you can do the more difficult things. If you intend to learn how to solve a new kind of mathematical problem during a study session, begin by working out some problems you already know how to solve. If you want to learn new vocabulary words for a foreign language course, start by reviewing the words you already know. In other words, begin most of your study sessions by reviewing something you have learned previously. This practice not only eases you into the study session, but helps you learn the things you need to learn.

In Lesson 7 you will learn how to survey books and chapters in books. Surveying is the way to "warm up" to a reading assignment. Since many college assignments are reading assignments, the survey is a basic way to get started in most study sessions.

DECIDING WHEN TO STUDY WITH SOMEBODY ELSE

Under most circumstances it is best to study alone rather than with another person, but there are some exceptions. Consider these exceptions whenever you ask yourself, "Is it a good idea to study with somebody else?"

1. *When you wish to review for a test,* it might be a good idea to review with friends who have learned as much as you have learned. These friends may not know some of the things you know, but their knowledge should be about equal to yours because, when you are reviewing for a test, you want to spend your time learning, not teaching. However, it *is* a good idea to study with people who are willing to teach you.
2. *When you wish to master a skill,* you will find it useful to teach that skill to another person. You do not teach somebody something to prepare yourself for a test, because if you know something well enough to teach it to another person, you already know it well enough to take a test on it. However, if you really want to become expert at solving mathematical or scientific problems, translating a foreign language into English, or other such abilities, try instructing someone else.
3. Studying can be a very lonely and isolating experience—so lonely that some people are prevented from learning when they study alone. *If you feel extremely lonely when you are studying,* you may find it helpful to study with a friend. It is best if the friend is studying the same thing you are studying, but sometimes even being with a person who is studying something else can be helpful in reducing feelings of isolation.

AVOIDING THE NEED FOR CRAMMING

Is it a good idea to cram? No, it is not a good idea to try to learn in a day or a week the things you should have spent a month learning. There are two reasons why this is so.

First, most things are learned best if they are practiced over a long period of time rather than over a short time span. Common sense tells you that a person will learn to be a better driver by taking thirty hours of driving instruction in thirty hour-long lessons spread over six weeks than by taking thirty hours of instruction crammed into one week.

The same is true of almost anything that is to be learned. There are only a few exceptions: (1) trying to find the solution to a complex problem, and (2) writing a paper. If it will take you two hours to find the solution to a complex problem, then it is better to set aside two hours than to set aside four half-hour sessions. If it will take you three hours to write a paper, you will be better off setting aside three hours to write it than giving yourself three one-hour periods. With these exceptions, you will learn best if you stretch your learning out over a long period of time, rather than cram too much learning into a short time period.

The second problem with cramming is that when people cram, they usually feel guilty that they did not start studying earlier. They are pressed for time; and, being pressed for time, they worry about how well they will do on the test. These feelings interfere with learning. It simply is not possible to learn efficiently when feeling guilty, pressed for time, and worried about how you will do on a test. Information learned under such conditions is quickly forgotten.

Despite recognizing the problems involved with cramming, even the best-organized students sometimes find themselves with less time to study than they would ideally like to have. The next lesson, which describes how to study, ends with a suggestion on how to spend your study time when you have very little of it.

REMEMBERING INFORMATION FOR TESTS

Psychologists have discovered that information is easier to learn and remember when it is organized than when it is not organized. Many of the lessons in this book are designed to help you develop organizational skills so you can arrange information for easier learning. However, even after you have used all the suggestions given in this book, there still will be times when you will have difficulty learning something you want to remember and will ask yourself, "How can I learn to remember things?" At those times it might be helpful to use a mnemonic (ni-mon'ik) device. *Mnemonic* means "to help the memory," and a *mnemonic device* is something that helps you remember. Two such devices that are widely used by students are called mnemonic acronyms and mnemonic sentences.

Mnemonic acronyms are words made from the initial letters of other words. A student wanted to learn the following list of rules for taking tests:

> Read all directions.
> Easy questions are answered first.
> Answer all questions.
> Proofread your answers.

The student made a mnemonic acronym, REAP, to help him remember the list. The *R* in *REAP* recalled "Read all directions," and so on.

Make a mnemonic acronym for the four steps for study that are given in the next lesson. They are:

> Survey before you read.
> Organize what you read.
> Anticipate test questions.
> Recite and review.

Mnemonic sentences are sentences such as the following:

Every good boy does fine.

This is probably the best known of all mnemonic sentences. It is used to remember the notes on the lines of the musical staff. The *e* in *every* is for the note on the bottom line, the *g* in *good* is for the note on the second line, and so on:

Another well-known mnemonic sentence is this one, used to learn the sequence of the planets starting with the one nearest the sun and going to the one most distant from the sun:

My	Very	Earthy	Mother	Just	Served	Us	Nine	Pizzas.
e	e	a	a	u	a	r	e	l
r	n	r	r	p	t	a	p	u
c	u	t	s	i	u	n	t	t
u	s	h		t	r	u	u	o
r				e	n	s	n	
y				r		e		

You will understand the value of mnemonic devices better if you practice using one. Learn the mnemonic sentence for the planets and then test yourself by answering these questions:

1. Which planet is closest to the sun?
2. Which planet is seventh from the sun?
3. Which planets are on either side of Earth, and which of these is closest to the sun?
4. Which planets are on either side of Saturn, and which of these is farthest from the sun?

Memory experts claim that mnemonic sentences are easiest to remember when they are funny, fanciful, or as ridiculous as possible. According to this theory, even though both of the following sentences contain words that begin with the same letters, the second one will be easier to remember:

You may win at baseball.
Your mother wears Army boots.

It sort of makes sense, doesn't it?

Mnemonic devices such as these are powerful tools for implanting information in the memory. The more courses you take in college and the more you must remember, the more likely it is that you will construct mnemonic acronyms and mnemonic sentences for learning.

The major problem with mnemonic devices is that they are usually forgotten quickly. And when they are forgotten, the information they brought to mind is forgotten also. Overreliance on mnemonic devices is not true learning. True learning comes from having information well organized in your mind. That is why so much of this book is devoted to developing organizational skills and so little to mnemonic devices. Mnemonic devices should be used primarily when other learning methods fail.

Lesson 6. What Is Study?

The word *study* has several meanings, but the one that best describes most study that is done in college is the one given in *Webster's New Dictionary of Synonyms:*

> Study stresses continuity and closeness of attention; it usually also implies an aim such as the acquisition of knowledge, or the analysis of something that is complex or confusing.*

The purpose of this book is to help you develop good study habits by giving you practice that will help you learn how to pay attention and by giving you methods you can use to acquire knowledge and analyze complex and confusing information.

THE SOAR STUDY FORMULA

The procedures for efficient study are summarized in the steps of the SOAR study formula:

> <u>S</u>urvey before you read.
> <u>O</u>rganize what you read.
> <u>A</u>nticipate test questions.
> <u>R</u>ecite and review.

The entire second part of this book is devoted to helping you learn how you can use the steps of the SOAR study formula to study the courses you take in college. This lesson gives a brief explanation of the four steps so you will have a general idea of what constitutes an effective study program.

Step One: Survey Before You Read. *Surveying* involves previewing or getting an overview of what you will read before you actually read it.

Throughout your schooling you have been given assignments requiring you to read a certain number of pages in a book. Most students do these assignments by turning to the first page to be read and then reading until they reach the last page. It has been well established that this is a very inefficient way to go about reading most of the material that needs to be read in college.

Educational psychologists have found that the reading of a chapter is much more efficient if the reader first spends a few minutes looking through the chapter, examining the headings, pictures, diagrams, and so on, to get a general idea about the chapter before actually reading it. It is for this

---

* By permission. From Webster's New Dictionary of Synonyms © 1973 by G. & C. Merriam Co., Publishers of the Merriam-Webster Dictionaries.

reason that the survey technique is described in this book and most books that teach study skills to college students. It is a very simple, but very important, step in any study program.

Step Two: Organize What You Read. One of the best-known facts about human learning is that information is easiest to learn when it is organized in some meaningful way. A simple example will make this principle easy to understand. Two groups of students were given 90 seconds to learn a list of twenty words. One group studied the list arranged in random order while the other group studied the same list arranged in a meaningful organization. The lists appear as follows:

RANDOM LISTING FOR THE FIRST GROUP

tall, orange, French, comedy, apple, thin, strawberry, opera, fat, pear, English, drama, pretty, history, ballet, chemistry, short, grape, algebra, circus

ORGANIZED LIST FOR THE SECOND GROUP

tall	English	orange	comedy
thin	French	apple	ballet
fat	history	strawberry	drama
short	chemistry	pear	opera
pretty	algebra	grape	circus

The lists were taken away after 90 seconds, and the students were asked to write down as many of the words as they could remember. You will probably not be surprised to learn that, on the average, the students who studied the random list recalled only eight words, while the students who studied the organized list recalled an average of sixteen words. The recall of the second group was twice that of the first group simply because the good organization of the second list made that list easier to learn. Although you will not learn lists of words such as these in college, good organization of the things you need to learn will help you to learn them.

There are two basic ways in which you may organize information for study purposes: by marking textbooks and by making written notes. The basic purpose of *marking textbooks* is to make important information stand out so it can be found quickly and learned when being reviewed for a test. Figure 6.1 shows one way a page from a textbook might be marked for studying. You have probably discovered by now that many college students make various kinds of marks in their textbooks. Some students underline, some use colored pens, some make summarizing notes in the margins of books, and some use combinations of these methods. Lessons 8 and 21 explain various ways to mark textbooks. If you begin to mark your books, you will probably find that textbooks that are fairly easy to read can usually be marked during the first reading, but with textbooks that are difficult to understand, you do better to read them through once without doing any marking and then read them a second time to mark important information.

Some students do most of their studying from the marks they have made in their textbooks. However, most successful students probably find that

Figure 6.1 An Example of One Method to Use in Marking a Book. (From INTRO-DUCTION TO PSYCHOLOGY Sixth Edition by Ernest R. Hilgard, Richard C. Atkinson and Rita L. Atkinson copyright © 1975 by Harcourt Brace Jovanovich, Inc., and reprinted by permission of the publishers)

Organization and Memory

Memories are patterns of items, woven together by rules that impose varying degrees of *organization;* success in retrieval depends upon how much organization is present. When lists of words or other materials are studied, the greater the degree of organization that the learner can impose on the material, the better the subsequent recall (Mandler, 1974).

Experiment

A dramatic illustration of the effect of organization on memory is provided in the following experiment. The subjects were required to memorize four separate lists of words. For some subjects each of the word lists was presented on a slide in the form of a hierarchical tree, much like the example shown in Figure 8-12. The other subjects studied each of the lists for the same length of time, but the items in each list were arranged randomly on the presentation slide. When tested later, subjects recalled 65 percent of the words presented in a hierarchical organization, but only 19 percent of the same words presented in random arrangements. Further analysis of the data indicated that the subjects who were given the words in an organized form used the hierarchical arrangement as a retrieval scheme for generating recall.

Self-recitation During Practice

Importance

Recall during practice usually takes the form of reciting to oneself. Such self-recitation increases the retention of the material being studied. Suppose a student has two hours to study an assignment that can be read through in 30 minutes. Rereading the assignment four times is likely to be much less effective than reading it once and asking himself questions about the material he has read. He can then reread to clear up points that were unclear as he attempted to recall them. The generalization that it is efficient to spend a good fraction of study time in attempting recall is supported by experiments with laboratory learning as well as by experiments with school learning.

Experiment

The percentage of study time that should be spent in self-recitation depends on the material and the type of test for which one is preparing. However, the percentage may be higher than our intuitions might suggest. A well-known laboratory experiment indicates that the greatest efficiency in recall of historical material occurs when as much as 80 percent of the study time is devoted to self-recitation. The amount of information recalled increases in proportion to the percentage of study time spent in self-recitation.

Advantages

The self-recitation method in ordinary learning forces the learner to define and select what is to be remembered. In addition, recitation represents practice in the retrieval of information in the form likely to be demanded later on. That is, the learner tries to outline a history chapter or provide illustrations of operant conditioning in a fashion similar to what might be expected on an examination. The rule is to begin an active process of recall early in a study period. Time spent in active recall, with the book closed, is time well spent.

Figure 6.1 **(continued)**

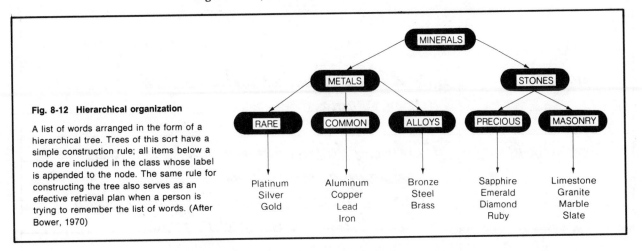

Fig. 8-12 Hierarchical organization

A list of words arranged in the form of a hierarchical tree. Trees of this sort have a simple construction rule; all items below a node are included in the class whose label is appended to the node. The same rule for constructing the tree also serves as an effective retrieval plan when a person is trying to remember the list of words. (After Bower, 1970)

written notes are the most useful aids to learning. Figure 6.2 gives an example of notes that can be used for studying. By examining used books in your college bookstore, you might discover that students mark books for studying, but it would be more difficult for you to discover on your own that good students also make notes for study purposes. Lessons 8 and 22 explain various ways to make notes for studying. Also, Lessons 14 through 20 will help you learn how to outline so you can develop skills needed for note taking.

Step Three: Anticipate Test Questions. Some students are almost always well prepared for tests because they are able to figure out what questions are likely to be on the tests. These students have learned how to anticipate test questions. They know that most college professors base their test questions on what is written in course textbooks or what is said in class lectures. They study their textbooks and notes, trying to figure out what questions might be asked about the material; then they study to learn the answers to the questions they anticipate.

Students in a psychology course might read a passage on Piaget's ideas about the stages of intellectual development. At some *subconscious* level every student who reads the passage assumes that a test question might be asked about it, but skillful students *consciously* anticipate specific questions and study to answer them. If the teacher of a psychology course gives essay tests, students might prepare to discuss completely Piaget's stages of intellectual development in a long, written answer. If the teacher gives multiple-choice tests, students might study the passage and imagine the different kinds of multiple-choice questions that could test their knowledge of the information, again preparing answers for the questions they anticipate.

Of the various ways to anticipate test questions the easiest is to turn textbook headings into questions. For example, the headings in Lesson 4 of this book could be turned into questions that might appear on a study skills test. The first one would be "What are the characteristics of good lecture notes?" To understand this technique, change the other headings in

Figure 6.2 An Example of One Way of Making Notes for Study. These notes are for learning chronological information in a history course.

1914, July 28	World War I begins when Austria declares war on Serbia
1914, August	1. Germany declares war on Russia and France 2. Germany enters Belgium 3. Japan declares war on Germany and Austria 4. First German air raid on Paris 5. British forces land in France
1915, February 18	Germans begin submarine blockade of Great Britain
1915, April 25	British and French troops land in Turkey
1915, May 17	Sinking of Lusitania brings U.S. to brink of war
1915, May 23	Italy declares war against Austria-Hungary
1916, August 28	Italy declares war on Germany
1916, December 18	U.S. President Woodrow Wilson submits his own peace proposals to the warring countries
1917, April 6	The U.S. declares war on Germany
1917, June 26	First U.S. troops land in France
1917, December 7	U.S. declares war on Austria
1918, January 8	U.S. President Woodrow Wilson outlines his "Fourteen Points" for peace in speech to Congress

Lesson 4 into questions, which you can then practice answering. You will learn more about anticipating test questions when you study Lessons 10, 11, and 12.

Step Four: Recite and Review. *Reciting* is the act of repeating information to yourself so it can be remembered and recalled; *reviewing* is the repetition of recitation until information has been completely learned. Without any fear of exaggeration, it is safe to say that *reciting is the single most important step in any study program.*

This very strong statement can be explained by an example or two. If you were taking an advanced mathematics course, you would learn how to solve new mathematical problems by working out the solutions to many problems on paper. This practice would be a form of recitation, because you would be working out problems for yourself so you could remember and recall how to solve similar problems in a test situation. It is not possible for most people to learn how to solve difficult mathematical problems without doing this kind of recitation. Similarly, if you were taking a Spanish, French, or German course to learn to write in one of these languages, you would learn to write the language fluently only if you practiced doing so. This, also, would be a form of recitation.

In most college courses recitation is not done with paper and pencil; it is done by repeating information aloud to oneself. But this is still recitation, and it is as important for learning information as it is for learning how to solve mathematical problems or how to write in a foreign language.

The great mass of information that supports the importance of recitation has been summarized by Hilgard, Atkinson, and Atkinson in their popular psychology textbook.* These writers state that reading an assignment four times is not as effective as reading it once, asking questions about it, and then attempting to recite the answers to the questions. They claim that there is sufficient research to support the generalization that a good proportion of all study time should be spent attempting to recall or recite answers to questions. They give two basic reasons for this:

1. Reciting forces learners to identify and select the information they wish to learn and remember.
2. Reciting provides practice in doing the thing that is required in a test-taking situation. For example, when a student recites all she can about the stages of intellectual development as classified by Piaget, she is doing very much the same thing she would do if called upon to answer questions about this information in a test.

SUMMARY OF THE SOAR STUDY FORMULA

Even if you used to believe that the best way to study is to read and reread your textbooks, you should now understand that this is *not* an efficient way to study. Experienced and successful students follow these steps to *study* reading assignments:

* Ernest R. Hilgard, Richard C. Atkinson, and Rita L. Atkinson, *Introduction to Psychology,* 6th ed. (New York: Harcourt Brace Jovanovich, Inc., 1975), p. 244.

1. They *survey before they read* by spending a few minutes looking through a chapter to get a general idea of its contents.
2. They *organize what they read* by marking their textbooks and making notes for study (marks in textbooks are used to find the information that will be put in notes).
3. They *anticipate test questions* that might be asked about information given in their textbooks and class lectures.
4. They use most of their study time to *recite and review;* they say information back to themselves so it can be remembered and recalled when they take tests.

These four steps require two or three readings of a textbook. If a chapter in a textbook is difficult to understand, read it once without making marks and mark it during the second reading; if it is easy to understand, mark it on the first reading. Once notes for study are made, you do not need to refer to the textbook again except to make additions and other improvements to notes that are being used for recitation. About one-half of your study time should be spent reading books, marking them, and making notes; the other half should be spent reciting.

If you have never studied in this way before, it may seem to be a very time-consuming way to study. Just the opposite is true; students who read textbooks through four times do not learn as much as students who read them once to mark them and a second time to make notes on them, and then spend the rest of their study time reciting. Your study in this book will help you understand how you can use the four steps for study to learn more efficiently in the college courses you take.

In Lesson 5 you were given two basic reasons why it is not a good idea to cram for tests and were promised a suggestion for how to use your study time when you have too little of it. Cramming is not advised, but if you wish to be able to cram, you must become expert at organizing what you read and anticipating test questions. When you can do these two things quickly, you are free to spend most of your study time reciting. Reciting is the means we use to remember and recall information. Most study time should be spent reciting, and reciting is done most effectively from well-organized notes.

Part 2. The SOAR Study Formula

STEP ONE:
SURVEY
BEFORE YOU READ

Lesson 7. Surveying Books and Chapters

STEP TWO:
ORGANIZE
WHAT YOU READ

Lesson 8. Marking Your Textbooks

Lesson 9. Making Written Notes

STEP THREE:
ANTICIPATE
TEST QUESTIONS

Lesson 10. Using Headings to Anticipate Test Questions

Lesson 11. Four Other Methods for Anticipating Test Questions

Lesson 12. Anticipating the Unexpected

STEP FOUR:
RECITE
AND REVIEW

Lesson 13. Reciting and Reviewing

In this part of the book you will practice the four steps of the SOAR study formula: "Survey before you read," "Organize what you read," "Anticipate test questions," and "Recite and review." These steps are organized into lessons as shown at the left. The suggested practice for Lessons 8 through 13 is based on the passages from college textbooks on pages 52–62. There is a multiple-choice test of the information in those passages that you may take to evaluate how well you learned to use the SOAR study formula.

The skills for step two, "Organize what you read," are more difficult to acquire than are the skills for the other steps in the SOAR study formula. Thus, the entire third part of this book is devoted to helping you learn the organizational skills that you can use to become more expert at marking your textbooks and making notes for studying. In this part of the book you will learn about surveying, anticipating test questions, reciting and reviewing, and *some* things about organizing what you read. In Part 3 you will learn more about organizational skills and ways to mark your textbooks and make notes on most kinds of information in them.

Lesson 7. Surveying Books and Chapters

Many students, when faced with a reading assignment in a textbook, turn to the page where the assignment begins and read through the assigned pages until they reach the end. This is *not* the best way to begin studying a reading assignment in a textbook! Experienced students know that the reading of an assignment can be done more efficiently if they spend a few minutes looking over all the pages of the assignment before beginning to read. They leaf through the pages, reading headings that describe the contents of the chapter; they examine pictures, tables, maps, or graphs; and, in general, they try to get an overview of what they will read before they start their careful reading. This technique is called *surveying,* and it is an excellent preparation for every reading assignment you have in college.

Any type of book may be surveyed, but the two forms provided in this lesson are for surveying textbooks. The word *textbook* as used here refers to the thick summarizing books that are usually used only in the study of school courses. For example, the books used to study business, sociology, and psychology are textbooks.

In some courses in college the texts may be novels, books of poetry, or a selected group of paperback books on any subject. Although these kinds of materials can be surveyed, the questions on the forms for this lesson were not written for surveying them. In addition, textbooks for English courses, foreign language courses, mathematics courses, and some secretarial courses are among other kinds of books that are not suitable for the surveys you will do for this lesson. Check with your instructor to make certain the books you survey are appropriate for the forms.

Textbook Survey Form 1

Part 1: Survey of a Book

The best source of information about the *title, author,* and *date of publication* is the *title page,* which is usually the first or second page in a book. The date of publication is on the back of the title page.

1. What is the title of the book?

   _____

2. Who is the author of the book?

   _____

3. In what year was the book published? _____

If a book has a *preface* or *introduction,* it will be in the front of the book.

4. Does the book have a preface? _____

5. Does the book have an introduction? _____

The *table of contents* is in the front of the book, usually immediately following the title page.

6. Examine the table of contents to see if the chapters are grouped together under a few major headings. If they are, list the major headings and indicate how many chapters there are under each major heading.

Major headings for chapters	Number of chapters
_____	_____
_____	_____
_____	_____
_____	_____
_____	_____
_____	_____

A *glossary* is a dictionary of difficult and technical words used in a textbook. If your book has a glossary, it is probably in the back of the book, but some books have a short glossary at the end of each chapter.

(continued)

7. If your book has a glossary, read the definitions of some of the words and estimate how many of them you know:

all of them   _____   about half   _____

most of them   _____   fewer than half _____

more than half _____   few of them   _____

A *subject index* is found at the end of a book. If there is an *author index,* it will come just before the subject index.

8. Does the subject index appear to be long, detailed, and complete?

_____

9. Does the book have a separate author index? _____

Bibliography, references, and *selected readings* all refer to listings of books and articles. They may appear in the backs of books, at the ends of chapters, or in both places.

10. Does the book have a bibliography, references, or selected readings?

_____

An *appendix* is comprised of additional materials placed at the end of a book. An appendix often contains interesting information, although one may not appear in all books.

11. If your book has an appendix, what kind of material or information has been placed in it?

_____

_____

_____

Part 2: Survey of a Chapter

The rest of the questions are to be answered by doing a survey of one chapter of your textbook.

12. Select a chapter in the textbook to survey. What is the title of the chapter you selected?

_____

(continued)

13. How many pages are there in the chapter? _____

14. How long do you estimate it would take you to read the chapter?

_____

15. If you wanted to divide the chapter into several parts for study purposes, it would be best to divide it into its natural major divisions. What are the titles of the major divisions in the chapter?

_____

_____

_____

_____

A *summary* may be found at the beginning or end of a chapter, but usually is at the end. If a chapter has a summary, it is a good idea to read it before reading the chapter, even if it appears at the end of the chapter.

16. Does the chapter have a summary? _____

Important words are often printed in a special kind of type that is darker or lighter than the other print on a page.

17. Are important words printed in a special kind of type? _____

Notes are of two basic types. One type, the *footnote,* is found by a raised number, such as the following numeral [1], or by an asterisk, *. The raised number or asterisk sends the reader to the bottom of the page. The other type, the *endnote,* is found by a number like the following: (41). The "41" refers the reader to a listing at the end of the chapter or at the end of the book.

18. Are there footnotes or endnotes in your book? _____

19. Are there questions, problems, or assignments at the end of the chapter?

_____

20. Check any of the following that you find in the chapter:

graphs _____   diagrams _____

tables _____   photographs _____

maps _____   other pictures _____

Textbook Survey Form 2

Part 1: Survey of a Book

The best source of information about the *title, author,* and *date of publication* is the *title page,* which is usually the first or second page in a book. The date of publication is on the back of the title page.

1. What is the title of the book?

   _____

2. Who is the author of the book?

   _____

3. In what year was the book published? _____

If a book has a *preface* or *introduction,* it will be in the front of the book.

4. Does the book have a preface? _____

5. Does the book have an introduction? _____

The *table of contents* is in the front of the book, usually immediately following the title page.

6. Examine the table of contents to see if the chapters are grouped together under a few major headings. If they are, list the major headings and indicate how many chapters there are under each major heading.

Major headings for chapters	Number of chapters
_____	_____
_____	_____
_____	_____
_____	_____
_____	_____
_____	_____

A *glossary* is a dictionary of difficult and technical words used in a textbook. If your book has a glossary, it is probably in the back of the book, but some books have a short glossary at the end of each chapter.

(continued)

7. If your book has a glossary, read the definitions of some of the words and estimate how many of them you know:

all of them   _____   about half   _____

most of them   _____   fewer than half   _____

more than half   _____   few of them   _____

A *subject index* is found at the end of a book. If there is an *author index,* it will come just before the subject index.

8. Does the subject index appear to be long, detailed, and complete?

_____

9. Does the book have a separate author index? _____

Bibliography, references, and *selected readings* all refer to listings of books and articles. They may appear in the backs of books, at the ends of chapters, or in both places.

10. Does the book have a bibliography, references, or selected readings?

_____

An *appendix* is comprised of additional materials placed at the end of a book. An appendix often contains interesting information, although one may not appear in all books.

11. If your book has an appendix, what kind of material or information has been placed in it?

_____

_____

_____

Part 2: Survey of a Chapter

The rest of the questions are to be answered by doing a survey of one chapter of your textbook.

12. Select a chapter in the textbook to survey. What is the title of the chapter you selected?

_____

© 1979 by Houghton Mifflin Company

(continued)

13. How many pages are there in the chapter? _____

14. How long do you estimate it would take you to read the chapter?

_____

15. If you wanted to divide the chapter into several parts for study purposes, it would be best to divide it into its natural major divisions. What are the titles of the major divisions in the chapter?

_____

_____

_____

_____

A *summary* may be found at the beginning or end of a chapter, but usually is at the end. If a chapter has a summary, it is a good idea to read it before reading the chapter, even if it appears at the end of the chapter.

16. Does the chapter have a summary? _____

Important words are often printed in a special kind of type that is darker or lighter than the other print on a page.

17. Are important words printed in a special kind of type? _____

Notes are of two basic types. One type, the *footnote,* is found by a raised number, such as the following numeral [1], or by an asterisk, *. The raised number or asterisk sends the reader to the bottom of the page. The other type, the *endnote,* is found by a number like the following: (41). The "41" refers the reader to a listing at the end of the chapter or at the end of the book.

18. Are there footnotes or endnotes in your book? _____

19. Are there questions, problems, or assignments at the end of the chapter?

_____

20. Check any of the following that you find in the chapter:

graphs _____ diagrams _____

tables _____ photographs _____

maps _____ other pictures _____

Lesson 8. Marking Your Textbooks

This lesson will *introduce* ways to mark your textbooks to make them more useful when you study for tests. Textbooks are usually marked by underlining, highlighting, or a combination of both techniques. *Underlining* is done with pen or pencil, usually with the aid of a ruler; *highlighting* is done with special felt-tipped pens that contain watercolor ink. An example of an underlined textbook page appears in Figure 8.1; highlighting is explained later in this lesson.

Most study skills experts advise students to mark their textbooks because marking forces students to concentrate on their reading and helps ensure that they will find the things they want to learn. Whether one underlines or highlights is a matter of personal preference; perhaps you should try both methods to discover which one you prefer.

If you come from a high school where you were not allowed to mark in your books, it may be difficult for you to start highlighting or underlining your college texts. However, you should know that experienced students *do* mark their books and find their markings extremely helpful when they study. In a marked textbook it is easy to find at a glance the points to be learned.

If you can buy new, unmarked books, try to do so, so that you can mark them yourself as you read. If you purchase a used book, buy one with no markings or with very few markings. Just as it is difficult to study from another student's lecture notes, it is also difficult to read a book that has another student's markings in it.

The highlighting and underlining practice in this lesson is designed to give you an efficient way to find and learn the meanings of the many new words you will need to learn in your college courses. Textbooks, of course, contain many other kinds of information in addition to the meanings of important words, and methods of marking other kinds of information are explained in Lesson 21. But since one primary purpose of college courses is to teach students the meanings of words that are important to a subject, it is essential that you have a good way to find and learn such information.

The rules for underlining are given first, followed by the rules for highlighting. You may study both methods, or only the one you intend to practice and use.

**HOW TO UNDERLINE
TERMINOLOGY**

Here, in brief, are the rules that explain how to underline terminology:

Rule 1: Circle terminology.
Rule 2: Underline definitions.
Rule 3: Draw a line alongside examples.

Figure 8.1 A Textbook Passage That Is Marked Using the Rules for Underlining Given in This Lesson. The markings include marginal notes, which you will learn to write when you study Lesson 21. (From INTRODUCTION TO PSYCHOLOGY Sixth Edition by Ernest R. Hilgard, Richard C. Atkinson and Rita L. Atkinson copyright © 1975 by Harcourt Brace Jovanovich, Inc., and reprinted by permission of the publishers)

Transfer of Learning

An important issue in optimizing learning is the extent to which the learning of one thing facilitates the learning of something else. If everything we learned was specific to the situation in which it was learned, the amount of learning that would have to be crammed into a lifetime would be phenomenal. Fortunately, most learning is readily transferable, with some modification, to a number of different situations.

Positive Transfer

The influence that learning one task may have on the subsequent learning of another is called transfer of learning. The term positive transfer is used when learning one task does facilitate learning another. If one is a good tennis player, it is easier to learn to play squash; this is positive transfer. But transfer is not always positive; when interference occurs, we have negative transfer.

Negative Transfer

There are numerous examples of negative transfer in everyday life. When driving a car with automatic transmission after having been accustomed to one with a stick shift, we may find ourselves depressing a nonexistent clutch pedal. When changing from a pedal-brake to a hand-brake bicycle, we may still try to press back on the pedal when we have to stop quickly. And the transition from driving on the right-hand side of the street to the British procedure of driving on the left is difficult for many American visitors to Great Britain. The original habit is so overlearned that even after driving successfully on the left for some time, an individual may revert to right-side driving when required to act quickly in an emergency.

Doctrine of Formal Discipline

Importance of Transfer of Learning

The problem of transfer of learning has been historically of great concern to educators. For them it constitutes the very important practical question of how the school curricula should be arranged to ensure maximum positive transfer. Does learning algebra help in the learning of geometry? Which of the sciences should be taught first to ensure maximum transfer to other science courses?

One of the earliest notions of transfer of learning, prevalent among educators around the turn of the century, maintained that the mind was composed of faculties that could be strengthened through exercise, much as individual muscles can be strengthened. This notion, known as the doctrine of formal discipline, was advanced in support of keeping such studies as Latin and Greek in the high school curriculum. It was argued that the study of Latin, for example, trains a student's powers of self-discipline, reasoning, and observation.

Doctrine is not true

The doctrine of formal discipline has been largely discredited by experiments. Some transfer does take place, but it depends much less on formal mental training than on learning for a specific purpose. For example, the study of Latin does indeed improve the understanding of English words, but only those with Latin roots. It does not improve the understanding of words of Anglo-Saxon origin. And the extent to which improvement occurs depends upon the way the Latin is taught: the gain in English vocabulary is much greater when the course is taught with emphasis on word derivation than when taught by more conventional methods.

Figure 8.2 Sample Underlined Passages. In highlighting these passages, you would place pink highlighting where words are circled and yellow highlighting where lines are drawn.

1

Reinforcement refers to the thing that strengthens the possibility that a particular behavior will occur again. For example, one psychologist encouraged the behavior of lever pushing in rats by using the reinforcement of food—every time the rats pushed a lever they received a food pellet. If you are pleasant to a friend every time she calls you on the telephone, you are using reinforcement to strengthen her behavior of calling you.

2

Socialization refers to the process by which one selects from all the possible behaviors those behaviors that are appropriate to the people in one's surroundings. You probably dress the way you do because it is the way people around you dress. There are over a hundred sounds made in human speech around the world, but through socialization you selected the behavior of using only the forty or so sounds in your language and not the other speech sounds.

3

Validity and reliability are both important to tests. Validity refers to the extent to which a test measures whatever it is supposed to measure. For example, if your history professor gave you a test of what you studied in his course, the test would be valid if it measured how much history you learned. Reliability, on the other hand, refers to the extent to which a test consistently measures whatever it is supposed to measure. If third-graders scored third-grade on a reading test on May 1, they would score third-grade on the same test on June 2, if the test were reliable.

Terminology refers to words that are used in a particular field of study. A *definition* is a statement of the meaning of a word or term. And an *example* is something selected to show the general characteristics of persons, places, or things indicated by a word or term.

In Figure 8.2 you will find three examples of how the rules for underlining are used to solve the problems for this lesson. Note that the circled words in the first and second passage were printed in italic type, but that no words were printed in special type in the third passage in Figure 8.2. Also, note in Figure 8.2 that the words *reinforcement, socialization, validity,* and *reliability* appear more than one time in the passages, but that they are circled only once. The reason terms are circled only once is that the circling is intended to signal *one* thing to be learned. If you mark the same term two or three times, it will appear that you have two or three things to learn instead of just one.

HOW TO HIGHLIGHT TERMINOLOGY

The rules for highlighting are very similar to those for underlining.

Rule 1: Mark terminology in pink (instead of circling it).
Rule 2: Mark definitions in yellow (instead of underlining them).
Rule 3: Draw a yellow line alongside examples (instead of a pen or pencil line).

Many students prefer highlighting to underlining because (1) highlighting makes important points more prominent on the page and (2) it is possible to highlight neatly without using a ruler. To understand the advantages of highlighting, mark the sample passages in Figures 8.1 and 8.2 with pink and yellow highlight pens. Place pink on words that are circled; place yellow over underlined words and over lines drawn alongside the passages.

PRACTICE WITH UNDERLINING OR HIGHLIGHTING

Practice underlining or highlighting using the passages from English, speech, business, psychology, and advertising textbooks at the end of this lesson. In most of these passages, the words you will circle or mark in pink are printed in *italic* type. Sometimes, however, the important words in textbooks are not printed in special type. Since it is often difficult to find terms being explained in passages when they are not printed in special type, the following procedure is suggested for doing the problems: *Decide in class which terms should be circled or marked in pink. Circle or mark these terms in pink in class before you attempt to enter the marks for definitions and examples on your own outside of class.* Also, some of the practice passages had headings over them in the textbooks from which they were taken. So *after you have underlined or highlighted a passage, write a heading for the passage on the line above the passage.*

It would be best if pages 52–62 are *not* torn from this book. The passages on these pages are needed to solve problems in Lessons 12 and 30, and they may be used in ways described at the ends of Lessons 9 and 13.

Class Practice

Marking English Textbook Passages

Solve these problems using the underlining or highlighting directions given in Lesson 8.

1. _____

A simile is an analogy in which two dissimilar things are shown to be alike, at least in one respect. In a simile, the word *like* or *as* is used. For example:

> "*Words are like leaves,*
> And where they most abound
> Much fruit of sense beneath
> Is rarely found. . . .
>
> "But *true expression,*
> *Like the unchanging sun*
> Clears and improves
> Whate'er it shines upon."

ADDISON, "Essay on Criticism"

Passages 1–7 are from Burmeister, READING STRATEGIES FOR SECONDARY SCHOOL TEACHERS, 1974, Addison-Wesley, Reading, Mass.

2. _____

Metaphors, like similes, are analogies, but the word _like_ or _as_ is not used.

> They are two peas in a pod.
> Theresa is a vegetable.
> He is a peacock.
> "Merry larks are ploughmen's clocks."
> "All the world's a stage."
> "Dry leaves are little brown kites riding the wind."
> "The clouds are fairy castles in the sky."

3. _____

Personification is the technique of representing a thing or an animal as a person. For example:

> The flames ate the house.
> Fear lit flames of horror in her eyes.
> Money talks.
> The ocean threatens with the voice of an angry giant.
> The pages of my book speak to me with many voices.

4. _____

A euphemism is a pleasant term for what may be a very unpleasant idea. Since the idea is unpleasant, the euphemism remains a euphemism only for a time and then it, too, becomes unpleasant, and a new euphemism is needed.

Note the names for women's sizes: junior, misses, women's half-sizes, petites. Women's blouses are sized large, so that almost anyone can take size 12, 14, or 16, but skirts are smaller, so that most can take size 8, 10, or 12. Stretch stockings are not sized small, medium, large, and extra large, but short, average, long, and extra long. This pleases milady, for no woman wants to be considered extra large, but extra long is fine.

5. _____

We all have two types of vocabularies—_receptive_ and _expressive_. Our receptive vocabulary is composed of the words we recognize through reading and listening. This vocabulary is usually several times larger than our expressive vocabulary, which is made up of the words we use when we speak and write. Our total vocabulary is composed of the words we recognize and/or use in receptive and expressive ways.

6. _____

When we talk about the denotation of a word, we are talking about the literal meaning of the word. If the word has a physical referent, that object represents the denotation. The denotation of the word _cat,_ for example, is a four-legged animal, usually with a tail. The denotation of the word *lemon* is a small, yellow citrus fruit. The denotation of *green* is the color we call green.

7. _____

Denotations are very different from connotations, for connotations of words are interpretive meanings—poetic, emotional, colored. Consider the meaning of the word *cat* in the following sentence: Mrs. Glowgruber is a *cat*. What does *lemon* mean in: This T.V. is a *lemon*. And what is the meaning of *green* in: Leslie turned *green* when she heard Joanna had won. Can you think of other ways of using these same three words *connotatively*?

Assignment 1   *Marking Speech Textbook Passages*

Solve the following problems using the underlining or highlighting directions given in Lesson 8.

8. _____

Speeches are more interesting and easier to understand when they include good *examples*. Examples not only help people visualize something they have not experienced themselves, but can also arouse appropriate emotional reactions in an audience.

An example is something selected to show the general characteristics of anything that exists in the real world or in the imagination. Macaroni is an example of pasta; being deserted by his father is an example of a tragic event in the early life of Alexander Hamilton; dreaming about being a movie star is an example of a fantasy many people have.

9. _____

Examples are of two basic types: illustrations and instances. *Illustrations* are long and complete examples that usually include many details. In a speech about the difficulties of establishing a successful career in the theater, a speaker might select one or two well-known actors and illustrate the subject of the lecture by giving detailed accounts of the difficulties these famous people had in becoming established as stars. If speaking about how travel can be an educational experience, a speaker who has been to the University of Virginia and Monticello might illustrate this point by giving detailed reports of how such visits could result in developing a deeper appreciation of Thomas Jefferson, who designed structures at these places.

Instances are short examples that usually include less detail than illustrations. Since they are brief, it is usually necessary to include several instances to make a point convincing. A speaker who wanted to develop the idea that there are many advantages to living in New York City could use the following instances very effectively:

> If you enjoy any of the arts, New York City is the art center of the country.
> It is a great center for all sports and popular music.
> Any night of the week you may dine at an elegant restaurant or eat the food from any one of dozens of countries of the world in small, inexpensive restaurants.
> If there is something you want to buy, you can probably buy it in New York City.
> It is situated within an hour or two of some of the best beaches and most beautiful countryside in America.
> Boston, Philadelphia, and Washington, D.C., are some of the important centers that are a short drive from New York City.

(continued)

10. _____

Whenever you compare two things, you point out how they are alike; you make an analogy. Analogies are of two types: literal and figurative.

Literal Analogy. When you compare two teachers, two schools, two automobiles, two restaurants, or two friends, you are comparing two things in the same category and you create a *literal analogy*. For example:

> Whoppers contain one large piece of hamburger, but Big Macs contain two small pieces.
> Babe Ruth and Hank Aaron are both known for their home-run records in baseball.

Literal analogies need not be short. If you gave a speech comparing New York City to Boston, your high school to your college, or the game of football to the game of baseball, there would be many comparisons to make and you would construct a long literal analogy.

Figurative Analogy. When you compare a person to Mickey Mouse, your mother to an angel, or a person in fine physical condition to a well-tuned engine, you are comparing two things from different categories and you create a *figurative analogy*. For example:

> She is as gentle as a lamb.
> He is a real tiger.

These, like all similes and metaphors, are figurative analogies; they compare two things from different categories.

It is possible to create very long figurative analogies showing, for example, how life is like a baseball game or how some dogs live better than some people. However, since two things from different classes are always more different than they are alike, it takes a great deal of skill to construct good extended figurative analogies.

11. _____

Narration is simply the telling of a story—the giving of an account of what happened. When you tell the story of a movie you saw, describe what happened to you during a day at school or on a date, or give an account of events in your life, you are using narration. We never outgrow our appreciation for a good story, so the speaker who develops the ability to recount events in an interesting way has a powerful tool for captivating audiences.

12. _____

Exposition differs from narration in that its primary intention is to provide an explanation. When you explain to somebody how to get from one place to another, tell people why you did something, or pass on knowledge of how to do something, you are using exposition. In exposition we make things we know plain or understandable to others who do not know or understand them. In speech making a great deal of exposition would probably be used in speeches about safe driving, good places to hike, interesting things to do for free, or ways to behave when being interviewed for a job.

Assignment 2

Marking Business Textbook Passages

Solve the following problems using the underlining or highlighting directions given in Lesson 8.

13. _____

Property is of two basic types: real and personal. The primary difference between real and personal property is that real property must be transferred from owner to owner by a formal instrument that is recorded in a public office, while personal property need not be. Real property includes land, buildings on the land, mineral deposits beneath the land, bodies of water on the land, anything attached to the land (such as vegetation, fences, and oil wells), and the air above the land. By contrast, one's furniture, clothing, money, automobiles, and books are examples of personal property. These items may be transferred from owner to owner without the recording, in a public office, of the kind of formal instrument that is needed for the transfer of real property.

14. _____

Among the ways in which real and personal property may be acquired are inheritance, legacy, and accession. *Inheritance,* as used here, refers to ancestry and to the acquisition of property under the laws of inheritance that are in effect in the state where a person lives. These laws specify who will receive the property of a person who dies leaving no will and who may not be excluded from receiving such property. Property is acquired by *legacy* when it is so specified in the properly executed will of a person who has died.

People often confuse inheritance and legacy. If you receive property when a friend dies, you receive it by legacy, not inheritance. You cannot inherit property from a person to whom you are not related. Inheritance laws differ from state to state. In some states a spouse cannot be disinherited, but children can be. It would be worthwhile to investigate the inheritance laws in the state where you live.

You acquire property by *accession* when there is an increase in something you already own. If you plant an apple tree and it bears fruit, the fruit is yours by right of accession; if your dog has puppies or your cat has kittens, the progeny belong to you by right of accession. Similarly, farmers are entitled to increases in their herds or crops because of the accession laws.

15. _____

Automobile insurance is designed to provide against losses that might occur to an automobile and its contents (including passengers) or to objects and persons that are outside the automobile.

Protection for one's automobile, its contents, and passengers is provided by fire and theft insurance, collision insurance, and medical payments insurance. *Fire and theft insurance* protects automobile owners from losses that might arise if their car is damaged by fire or a flying object, or if their car or its contents are stolen. If a car is damaged by a collision with a

(continued)

moving or stationary object, the resulting damage to the car may be covered by *collision insurance*. *Medical payments insurance* protects drivers and their passengers if they are injured while they are inside the automobile.

Protection for people and objects outside one's automobile are provided by public liability insurance and property-damage liability insurance. *Public liability insurance* protects drivers when their automobile causes bodily harm to persons outside the car, and *property-damage liability insurance* protects them if their automobiles should damage any property of others, including cars belonging to others.

16. _____

The important people in any court action are the plaintiff and the defendant. The *plaintiff* is the person who initiates a court action—the party to whom a wrong was allegedly done. The *defendant* is the accused—the one who allegedly did the wrong. If you purchased a faulty piece of merchandise and the company that sold it to you refused to refund your money or provide you with an acceptable replacement, you might take the company to court. In such an instance you would be the plaintiff (injured party) and the company would be the defendant (party accused of injuring you).

Assignment 3

Marking Psychology Textbook Passages

Solve the following problems using the underlining or highlighting directions given in Lesson 8.

17. _____

Premature birth is another phenomenon that seems to be predictive of the child's later development. The definition of prematurity should be in terms of the number of weeks of gestational age. An infant born at less than 37 weeks of gestational age (time since fertilization) is classified premature; one born between 37 and 40 weeks would be classified as normal. However, it is difficult to obtain information on the time of conception, and most scientists use the child's birth weight as the index of prematurity. When birth weight is used, an infant born under 5½ pounds is regarded as premature, and an infant born under 4 pounds is classified as severely premature.

18. _____

During the preschool years, sex-typing figures prominently in the socialization of the child. Most parents pay considerable attention to the sex-appropriateness of their child's behavior, rewarding responses that are appropriate to his sex and discouraging those that are not. Thus, parents are likely to encourage a boy to "fight back" if attacked by a peer, but they are more likely to punish this kind of behavior in their daughter (70).* If a preschool girl cries after losing a game, this reaction is likely to be accepted as appropriate for the "weaker sex," but a boy who shows tears is likely to be reminded that "little men don't cry."

19. _____

One of the most commonly observed symptoms of psychological tension during the middle-childhood years is the tic. "A tic is a repetitious, involuntary, and seemingly purposeless movement of interconnected muscles" (50, 118).* Usually tics involve repeated motor responses of the face, neck, and head, of which the child is largely unaware; the actions may include blinking of the eyes, nose-wrinkling, throat-clearing, yawning, shoulder-shrugging, head-shaking, and the like. Tics frequently are symptoms of repressed needs and conflicts, and sometimes the nature of a tic serves as a clue to the underlying conflict.

(*continued*)

* The number in parentheses refers the reader to a bibliography at the end of the book from which this passage was taken. This type of note is described in Part 2 of the Textbook Survey Form on page 43.

Passages 17–19 are from Mussen, Conger, and Kagan, CHILD DEVELOPMENT AND PERSONALITY, Fourth Edition, 1974, Harper & Row Publishers. Passages 20–23 are from INTRODUCTION TO PSYCHOLOGY Fifth Edition by Ernest R. Hilgard, Richard C. Atkinson and Rita L. Atkinson copyright © 1971 by Harcourt Brace Jovanovich, Inc., and reprinted by permission of the publishers.

20. _____

Many incentives are at once desirable and undesirable, both positive and negative. Candy is delicious, but also fattening. Going off for a weekend of skiing is fun, but the consequences of lost study time can be anxiety producing. The attitude toward a goal at once wanted and not wanted, liked and disliked, is called an *ambivalent* attitude. Ambivalent attitudes are very common: the child runs away from home to escape parental domination, only to come running back to receive parental protection; his attitude toward his parents is ambivalent. Another child enjoys school, but looks forward to vacation.

21. _____

Whenever a person's progress toward a desired goal is blocked, delayed, or otherwise interfered with, we say he encounters frustration. The word "frustration" has sometimes been used to refer to an emotional state instead of to an event. That is, as a consequence of blocked goal-seeking a person becomes confused, baffled, and annoyed; if we were to ask him how he feels he would probably say he felt angry and frustrated. He is thus equating frustration with an unpleasant emotional state. In this book, however, we shall hold to the meaning of frustration as the *thwarting circumstances,* rather than their consequences.

22. _____

Frustration often leads to aggression against the individual or object that is the source of the frustration. In ordinary play situations, when one small child takes a toy from another child, the second is likely to attack the first in an attempt to regain the toy. For many adults the aggression may be verbal rather than physical: the victim of a slighting remark usually replies in kind. The anger engendered when one is blocked tends to find expression in some kind of direct attack.

23. _____

However the aggression comes about, some children and some adults develop strong tendencies to injure themselves or others. The extreme forms have been given names: *sadism,* for the extreme motive to pain others; *masochism,* for the extreme motive to inflict pain upon oneself. In some forms of sadism and masochism the satisfaction to the aggressive person appears to be sexual in nature, illustrating how the strands from different motivational dispositions may become intertwined.

Assignment 4

Marking Advertising Textbook Passages

Solve the following problems using the underlining or highlighting directions given in Lesson 8.

24. _____

The decision of someone to buy a product is the end effect of many influences. Some of these may reach back to his cultural heritage (as might his food preferences). The study of man's cultural heritage is the province of the *anthropologist.* A man's decision may have been shaped by "the right thing to do" among his friends (see how alike they are in dress). The study of man as part of a group is the field of the *sociologist.* A man's action may be a direct result of his own goals and desires (as in buying a particular car). Man's reaction to his drives is the *psychologist's* zone of study. These disciplines often overlap, but they are all part of the behavioral sciences.

25. _____

There are three sets of dates of which to be aware in magazine scheduling: the *cover date,* the date appearing on the cover; the *on-sale date,* on which a magazine is issued (the January issue of Esquire is on sale December 3, important to know in scheduling); and the *closing date,* on which all material must be in the hands of the publisher to be included in a given issue. All dates are expressed in relation to the cover date.

26. _____

Total circulation is the actual number of copies sold by a publication, as revealed by its Audit Bureau of Circulation statement or other verified reports. *Primary circulation* represents the number of households who paid for the magazine, on newsstand or by subscription. *Pass-along circulation* is aptly termed to represent the readership of a magazine by people who had asked, "When you're through with that magazine, could I have it?" Such circulation may be quite extensive. Pass-along circulation also includes magazines read in the waiting rooms of physicians and dentists, and in beauty shops and barber shops.

27. _____

A trademark invariably consists of, or includes, a word or name by which people can speak of the product—"Do you have *Dutch Boy* paint?" That word or name is also called a *brand name.* A trademark may, but does not have to, include some pictorial element.

    A *trade name,* on the other hand, is the name under which a company does business. *General Mills,* for example, is the trade name of a company making a cake mix whose trademark (not trade name) is *Betty Crocker.* The terms *trademark* and *trade name* are often confused.

(*continued*)

Passages 24–30 are from Kleppner, ADVERTISING PROCEDURE, Sixth Edition, copyright 1973, Prentice-Hall, Inc. Used by permission.

28. _____

Direct-response Advertising. This describes any advertising that asks the reader for a prompt response to the advertisement, with his name and address. Typical uses of direct-response advertising are (1) selling merchandise or a service directly; (2) soliciting inquiries that will be followed up at home or in the office by a salesman, or by mail; (3) soliciting requests for a catalog (from which the recipient can subsequently order); and selling subscriptions or enrolling members in a club, for instance a book or record club.

Direct-response advertising uses a great variety of media—magazines, newspapers, television, radio, matchbook covers, paperback books, and direct mail.

29. _____

Mail-order Advertising. This is the form of direct-response advertising used in the marketing of goods directly from seller to buyer without recourse to a retail establishment, dealer, or salesman. Many media are used for mail-order advertising, as cited above. *Mail-order advertising,* which represents a way of selling, should not be confused with *direct-mail advertising,* representing the use of a medium.

30. _____

Direct-mail Advertising. This branch of direct-response advertising is the designation of any advertising sent through the U.S. mail, or by "independent postal services," which are currently the object of experiments in various cities. Direct mail is a medium in which the reader is usually asked to return a card, order form, application blank, or even a roll of exposed film—in other words, to take some action.

Lesson 9. Making Written Notes

Some students do most of their studying from underlining or highlighting in their textbooks. However, most successful students probably find that it is written notes, not marks in textbooks, that are the most useful tools for learning. During their first term in college most people become aware that experienced students make various kinds of marks in their textbooks; this realization may come from examining used textbooks in the bookstore or observing people studying in the library. Therefore, it is usually relatively easy for most new college students to understand the importance of learning to mark textbooks. On the other hand, it is more difficult for first-year students to discover on their own that successful college students do much of their studying from written notes. Students' written notes are not for sale in bookstores, and if other students are observed writing in the library, there is no way of knowing whether they are making written notes for study purposes.

However, the only reason that most successful students mark their textbooks with underlining or highlighting is so they can easily find the information they want to learn and put into written notes for studying. This point is illustrated by the underlined textbook passage in Figure 9.1 and the notes made for it in Figure 9.2. As the student read about transfer of learning and the doctrine of formal discipline in her psychology textbook, she marked the passage as shown in Figure 9.1. Later she made the notes in Figure 9.2, and she will study from the notes, not the textbook. If you compare the marked passage to the notes, you can understand that it would be much easier to learn about transfer of learning and the doctrine of formal discipline from the notes than it would be from the marked textbook.

If serious students do not make written notes for study, it is usually because (1) they have not discovered how helpful written notes can be for study or (2) they do not have the skills necessary to make notes easily and quickly. It is for the second reason—because many students lack organizational skills—that the entire third part of this book is devoted to helping you acquire the organizational skills that you need to make notes efficiently. This lesson gives some note-taking suggestions you can put to use even before you refine or develop your organizational skills by studying Part 3.

If you have never made notes from books, you should know that there are four important reasons for making notes on what you read.

1. The simple act of writing something down helps most people learn.
2. Sometimes explanations in textbooks can be confusing. The confusion is usually eliminated if you put the explanations into your own words. You cannot put something into your own words unless you really understand it. Thus, making written notes in your own words helps ensure that you understand the material.

Figure 9.1   An Example of a Textbook Page That Has Been Marked for Study. (From INTRODUCTION TO PSYCHOLOGY Sixth Edition by Ernest R. Hilgard, Richard C. Atkinson and Rita L. Atkinson copyright © 1975 by Harcourt Brace Jovanovich, Inc., and reprinted by permission of the publishers)

Transfer of Learning

An important issue in optimizing learning is the extent to which the learning of one thing facilitates the learning of something else. If everything we learned was specific to the situation in which it was learned, the amount of learning that would have to be crammed into a lifetime would be phenomenal. Fortunately, most learning is readily transferable, with some modification, to a number of different situations.

Positive Transfer — The influence that learning one task may have on the subsequent learning of another is called *transfer of learning.* The term *positive transfer* is used when learning one task does facilitate learning another. If one is a good tennis player, it is easier to learn to play squash; this is positive transfer. But transfer is not always positive; when interference occurs, we have *negative transfer.*

Negative Transfer — There are numerous examples of negative transfer in everyday life. When driving a car with automatic transmission after having been accustomed to one with a stick shift, we may find ourselves depressing a nonexistent clutch pedal. When changing from a pedal-brake to a hand-brake bicycle, we may still try to press back on the pedal when we have to stop quickly. And the transition from driving on the right-hand side of the street to the British procedure of driving on the left is difficult for many American visitors to Great Britain. The original habit is so overlearned that even after driving successfully on the left for some time, an individual may revert to right-side driving when required to act quickly in an emergency.

Doctrine of Formal Discipline

Importance of Transfer of Learning — The problem of transfer of learning has been historically of great concern to educators. For them it constitutes the very important practical question of how the school curricula should be arranged to ensure maximum positive transfer. Does learning algebra help in the learning of geometry? Which of the sciences should be taught first to ensure maximum transfer to other science courses?

One of the earliest notions of transfer of learning, prevalent among educators around the turn of the century, maintained that the mind was composed of faculties that could be strengthened through exercise, much as individual muscles can be strengthened. This notion, known as the *doctrine of formal discipline,* was advanced in support of keeping such studies as Latin and Greek in the high school curriculum. It was argued that the study of Latin, for example, trains a student's powers of self-discipline, reasoning, and observation.

Doctrine is not true — The doctrine of formal discipline has been largely discredited by experiments. Some transfer does take place, but it depends much less on formal mental training than on learning for a specific purpose. For example, the study of Latin does indeed improve the understanding of English words, but only those with Latin roots. It does not improve the understanding of words of Anglo-Saxon origin. And the extent to which improvement occurs depends upon the way the Latin is taught: the gain in English vocabulary is much greater when the course is taught with emphasis on word derivation than when taught by more conventional methods.

Figure 9.2   Study Cards for Learning Information About Transfer of Learning and the Doctrine of Formal Discipline

Back of study card for "transfer of learning"

The influence learning one thing has on learning something else.

1. Positive transfer is the process by which learning one thing helps learning other things. (Learning to drive a car helps learning to drive a truck.)

2. Negative transfer is the process by which learning one thing does not help learning other things. (Learning to drive on the right side of the road makes it difficult to drive on the left side of the road when visiting England.)

Back of study card for "doctrine of formal discipline"

* The mind can be made strong through exercise — it's like a muscle.

* Doctrine used to support teaching of Latin and Greek.

* Has been found untrue. Learning Latin does not strengthen mind. It helps develop vocabulary of words with Latin roots, but doesn't help with other words.

3. Sometimes textbooks contain so much information that the only way to isolate the things you want to know is to write them down in notes.
4. When you want to learn how ideas are related to each other, you will find that such relationships are easiest to learn when shown in notes.

STUDY NOTES

Study notes are written records of things to be learned that are systematically organized on pieces of paper. Three types of study notes are illustrated in this lesson to give you some idea of the various kinds of information that can be organized into notes for learning. Almost any information you might want to learn can be learned from study notes. The examples in this lesson are provided only to stimulate your thinking as to how you might organize other types of information you want to learn.

Terminology. In Figure 9.3 is an example of how terminology might be organized for learning in study notes. Please note exactly how the terminology is organized.

1. Items to be learned are listed on the lefthand side of the page.
2. Things to be learned about items are summarized on the righthand side.
3. A line is skipped between items.

Study notes are used by folding the page to cover the information to be learned. To understand this process, fold the sample study notes forward to the vertical line that separates the terms from their definitions. When the definitions are covered, read the term on the lefthand side of the page and attempt to recite the information that is concealed. Then you can uncover the definitions and check your progress.

Outlines. Many times it is necessary to learn the organization of ideas in an outline format. In Figure 9.4 you will find study notes made to learn about the stages of intellectual development according to Piaget. Note that the notes are very well organized. The four major stages stand out clearly, and Arabic numerals are used to label the important steps in the first two stages.

Historical Information. In history courses it is often important to know the sequence in which events occurred. Figure 9.5 shows how study notes may be organized for learning this kind of information. Note that the dates are listed in chronological order down the lefthand side of the page and that the events associated with the dates are listed on the righthand side of the page. This is a very effective way to organize this kind of information for efficient learning.

STUDY CARDS

Study cards are 3 × 5 index cards on which is written the same kinds of information that may be put into study notes. The single most important advantage of study cards over other note-taking methods is that once the information on a card has been learned, it may be separated from cards that have not been learned. Thus, study time may be spent learning things that have not been learned instead of constantly going over things that have

Figure 9.3 An Example of Study Notes Made for Learning Terminology—Fold Forward to the Vertical Line That Separates Terms from Definitions

simile	Figurative analogy using <u>like</u> or <u>as</u>. "Words are like leaves."
metaphor	Figurative analogy that does not use <u>like</u> or <u>as</u>. "Words are leaves."
personification	Giving human characteristics to a thing or animal. "Money talks."
euphemism	Pleasant way to speak of something unpleasant. "He passed away."
receptive vocabulary	Words we know when we read or listen.
expressive vocabulary	Words we use when we speak or write.
total vocabulary	All words in the expressive and receptive vocabularies.
denotation	Literal meaning of a word. "My <u>heart</u> is a muscle in my body."
connotation	Nonliteral, colored, or emotional meaning of a word. "She gave me her <u>heart</u>."
example	Something given to show the general characteristics of a person, place, or thing.
illustration	A long example.

Figure 9.4   An Example of Study Notes Made for Learning an Outline

Piaget's Stages of Intellectual Development

(I) Sensorimotor Stage (1 month to about 2 years)
 1. Reflexes (birth to 1 month) reflexes such as sucking become efficient.
 2. Primary Circular Reactions (1-3 months) repeats simple acts — like opening and closing fist
 3. Secondary Circular Reactions (4-6 months) repeats act for interesting response.
 4. Coordination of Secondary Reactions (7-10 months) begins to solve problems — knocks down pillow to find toy
 5. Tertiary Circular Reactions (11-18 months) tries new responses to objects
 6. Internal Mental Combinations (18 months) start of real intelligence

(II) Preoperational Stage (2 years to 7 years)
 1. Preconceptual Phase (2-4 years) child uses language but does not understand class membership
 2. Intuitive Thought Phase (4-7 years) constructs complex thoughts and groups objects into classes

(III) Concrete Operations Stage (7 to about 12 years)
 — Holds mental picture of path in mind. (e.g., path to school)
 — Understands conservation of mass
 — Understands serialization — arranges objects on a dimension (length, weight, etc.)

(IV) Formal Operations Stage (12 on)
 — Thought becomes more formal and systematic
 — Finds many solutions to a problem — considers alternatives

Figure 9.5   An Example of How Study Notes May Be Made for Learning Chronological Information for a History Class

1914, July 28	World War I begins when Austria declares war on Serbia
1914, August	1. Germany declares war on Russia and France 2. Germany enters Belgium 3. Japan declares war on Germany and Austria 4. First German air raid on Paris 5. British forces land in France
1915, February 18	Germans begin submarine blockade of Great Britain
1915, April 25	British and French troops land in Turkey
1915, May 17	Sinking of Lusitania brings U.S. to brink of war
1915, May 23	Italy declares war against Austria-Hungary
1916, August 28	Italy declares war on Germany
1916, December 18	U.S. President Woodrow Wilson submits his own peace proposals to the warring countries
1917, April 6	The U.S. declares war on Germany
1917, June 26	First U.S. troops land in France
1917, December 7	U.S. declares war on Austria
1918, January 8	U.S. President Woodrow Wilson outlines his "Fourteen Points" for peace in speech to Congress

already been learned. Three types of study cards are shown to give you an idea of kinds of information that might be studied from study cards.

Terminology. The sample study card in Figure 9.6 illustrates how cards may be made to learn terminology. Examine it to understand exactly how study cards are made.

1. The item to be learned is written in the center of the unlined side of the card.
2. The cards are numbered so they may be put back in correct order if they should become disorganized.
3. The information to be learned about the item is written on the lined side of the card. It is very important that after writing the item and number on the front of the card, you turn the card upside-down (flip it over) before writing information on the back.

Outlines. The study card in Figure 9.7 illustrates how a 3 × 5 index card might be used to reveal the relationship of ideas. The student who made this card could have made five terminology cards: one each for *rationalization, projection, substitution, sublimation,* and *compensation.* But instead, all the important information has been put in one convenient place on this single study card and has been arranged to help the student learn that sublimation and compensation are types of substitution.

Mathematical Information. The study card in Figure 9.8 is provided to emphasize that just about any information at all may be put on study cards for learning. In this case the study card is from a series of cards made to learn formulas in a statistics course.

**PRACTICE
IN MAKING STUDY NOTES
OR STUDY CARDS**

The best way to understand the value of study cards and study notes is *to make and use them for other college courses you are taking*. Therefore, if you are taking other college courses, it is suggested that you make study cards or study notes for learning at least thirty important pieces of information in one of your courses. If you do this, be certain that the notes you make can be used to study for a test you have not yet taken.

Also, you may make study cards or study notes to prepare for taking any or all of the following five tests:

1. a test on the information in Lessons 2 and 3
2. a test on the information about studying in Lessons 4 through 13
3. a test on the material on test-taking skills in Lessons 23 through 30
4. a test on information about English, speech, business, psychology, and advertising in the textbook passages for practicing underlining or highlighting in Lesson 8
5. a test of information in the passages used to practice outlining (Lesson 20), applying outlining skills to studying (Lesson 21), and making classification charts (Lesson 22)

The best way to understand the value of study notes or study cards is to make them and use them to prepare for tests.

Figure 9.6   An Example of a Study Card Made for Learning Terminology

The item to be learned is written boldly on the blank side of the card. This is card number 17 in a series of cards.

Loss Leader

17

Flip the card over so information on the back is written upside-down in relation to the words on the front of the card.

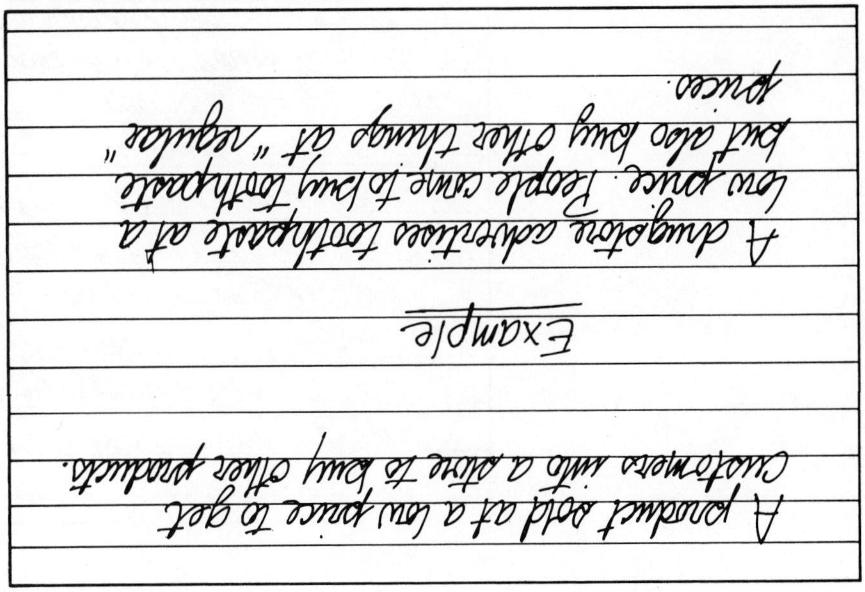

A product sold at a low price to get customers into a store to buy other products.

Example

A drugstore advertises toothpaste at a low price. People come to buy toothpaste but also buy other things at "regular" prices.

Figure 9.7   An Example of a Study Card Made for Learning an Outline

Front of card

29

Defense Mechanisms

Back of card

I. Rationalization- giving logical reasons for illogical behavior (blame low grade on teacher)

II. Projection- seeing our unacceptable characteristics in others but not in ourselves(see others' rudeness but not ours)

III. Substitution (useful)

   A. Sublimation- using socially acceptable activity to do what is not otherwise socially acceptable (play football to injure others)

   B. Compensation- making up for weakness in one area by being outstanding in another (poor athlete becomes very good student)

Figure 9.8   An Example of a Study Card Made for Learning a Formula for a Statistics Course

Front of card

6

Median

Back of card

$$\text{Median} = L + \left(\frac{n}{2} - \frac{\Sigma fb}{fw} \right) i$$

L = lower limit of interval in which median falls
n = number of observations in set
Σfb = sum of frequencies of observations below interval in which median falls
fw = frequency of observations within the interval containing the median
i = size of class interval

Lesson 10. Using Headings to Anticipate Test Questions

Headings in textbooks and headings or major thoughts in lecture notes summarize important information to be learned in a course. These headings or major thoughts are important tools to use for anticipating test questions.

TEXTBOOK HEADINGS

The following headings could summarize important information in a psychology textbook:

> Growth Patterns
> Early and Late Maturers

Most instructors ask questions about information and ideas printed in textbooks. Since headings in textbooks summarize the important information, it is only logical that in learning information summarized in the headings of your textbooks, you will have anticipated some of the questions that are likely to appear on your tests. For example, the two headings listed above might be turned into the following questions for a psychology test:

> What are the different growth patterns?
> What is the difference between early and late maturers?

The best way to appreciate the value of anticipating test questions from headings is simply *to start studying the headings in your textbooks today*. Then, when you take a test on a textbook that you have studied in this way, examine the test to estimate how many of the questions were similar to the ones you anticipated from the textbook headings.

If you follow this suggestion, you cannot help doing better on the next test you take. This is one of the easiest ways to anticipate test questions, and it is one of the best known and most widely used study methods of well-trained and experienced college students.

TEXTBOOK MARKINGS

When you use the suggestion in Lesson 8 to circle or mark words in pink, you are selecting important things to be learned. These markings can also be used to anticipate test questions. The words you circled or marked in pink when you did the problems for Lesson 8 are examples of the kinds of information covered in test questions.

PRACTICE WITH ANTICIPATING QUESTIONS

The headings (or markings you make) in any book you are studying may be used for anticipating test questions. The practice problems are designed to help you understand how you can use textbook headings to study for any course you take in college.

74

Class Practice

Headings and Test Questions

The problems for this exercise are based on headings that appear in this book. You are to decide what you should learn if a teacher should test you on information that appears under certain headings in this book. The following is a sample problem and its answer:

Heading: Finding Major Points in Lectures (page 21)
What should you learn?

1. Listen for information following pauses.
2. Listen for statements that are repeated.
3. Listen for introductory phrases, such as "the four points to consider are."

1. Heading: Deciding When to Study with Somebody Else (page 28)
   What should you learn?

   _____

   _____

   _____

   _____

   _____

   _____

2. Heading: Avoiding the Need for Cramming (page 28)
   What should you learn?

   _____

   _____

   _____

   _____

   _____

   _____

3. Heading: Remembering Information for Tests (page 29)
What should you learn?

_____

_____

_____

_____

_____

4. Heading: Step One: Survey Before You Read (page 32)
What should you learn?

_____

_____

_____

_____

_____

5. Heading: Step Four: Recite and Review (page 37)
What should you learn?

_____

_____

_____

_____

_____

Assignment 1

Headings and Test Questions

Select a textbook you are studying and use some headings in it to anticipate test questions.

Title of textbook: _____

Subject or course: _____

If you have no other textbooks, you may use the headings in this book for this assignment. Write the headings and the things you should learn on the lines provided.

1. Heading: _____

_____

What should you learn?

_____

_____

_____

_____

_____

_____

2. Heading: _____

_____

What should you learn?

_____

_____

_____

_____

_____

_____

3. Heading: _____

_____

(*continued*)

What should you learn?

_____

_____

_____

_____

_____

_____

4. Heading: _____

_____

What should you learn?

_____

_____

_____

_____

_____

_____

5. Heading: _____

_____

What should you learn?

_____

_____

_____

_____

_____

_____

Assignment 2

Headings and Test Questions

Select a textbook other than the one you used to do the problems for Assignment 1.

Title of textbook: _____

Subject or course: _____

If you have no other textbooks, you may use headings in this book to do this assignment. Write the headings and the things you should learn on the lines provided.

1. Heading: _____

_____

What should you learn?

_____

_____

_____

_____

_____

_____

2. Heading: _____

_____

What should you learn?

_____

_____

_____

_____

_____

_____

3. Heading: _____

_____

(continued)

What should you learn?

_____

_____

_____

_____

_____

_____

4. Heading: _____

_____

What should you learn?

_____

_____

_____

_____

_____

_____

5. Heading: _____

_____

What should you learn?

_____

_____

_____

_____

_____

Lesson 11. Four Other Methods for Anticipating Test Questions

Lesson 6 began with this definition of the word *study* from *Webster's New Dictionary of Synonyms:*

> Study stresses continuity and closeness of attention; it usually also implies an aim such as the acquisition of knowledge, or the analysis of something that is complex or confusing.*

This lesson describes ways to find all sorts of information to attend to, including complex or confusing information.

Students who know how to find all the information to be learned for a course are the ones who anticipate the questions that are likely to appear on tests. And students who anticipate questions that appear on tests usually do better on tests than other students. You may use the methods for anticipating questions on college tests to determine if you have mastered anything you want to learn in college, on a job, or on your own.

**METHOD ONE:
BE OBSERVANT IN CLASS**

You should observe carefully what your instructors do in class because they might well be giving clues about the questions you should expect on the tests they will give. Sometimes these clues are very clear and direct, as when teachers openly tell students to be ready to answer specific questions on a test. It may surprise you, but experienced teachers know that even when they announce specific test questions in class before a test, some students do not prepare to answer the questions. Apparently, these students cannot believe that a college professor would "give away" test questions. However, professors who do this are not giving anything away; they are only trying to make certain that students learn the things that they believe are vital to their subject matter. Therefore, pay very close attention whenever an instructor suggests you might be tested on specific information, and prepare yourself to be tested on it.

Whether or not instructors announce certain test questions before a test, all of them spend class time emphasizing those things they believe to be of special importance in their course content. Therefore, good class notes give very important clues as to the types of questions students should expect on tests. Please review Lesson 4 to make certain you understand how to take good lecture notes.

College professors have so many different ways in which they signal test questions to students that it is impossible to identify all of them. Here, however, are two behaviors that you should watch for:

---

* By permission. From Webster's New Dictionary of Synonyms © 1973 by G. & C. Merriam Co., Publishers of the Merriam-Webster Dictionaries.

1. When an instructor writes a person's name, a date, or a term, or draws a diagram, on the chalkboard, this is often a clue to a test question. Any such item should be copied down and marked for special attention in studying.
2. When teachers give special attention to some point of information that does not appear in the course textbook or that was given very little attention in the textbook, this is often a clue to a question that will be on a test.

To understand these suggestions better, study the test items the next time you take a test and try to recall how they are related to the things the professor did in class. Many questions on any instructor's test should be related to things said in class and things written on the chalkboard. If people in your class have already taken some college tests, *discuss* how questions on the tests were related to things the instructors did in class.

Few college professors limit their test questions to information printed in course textbooks. Most college professors feel that you should be conscientious about learning the things they teach in class sessions, too. However, even instructors who do not test you on the material covered in class will usually try to help you understand what information in the textbook is of special importance.

METHOD TWO:
PAY ATTENTION TO
CONFUSING INFORMATION

Most instructors want to include on tests some items that will be answered correctly only by the students who have studied most thoroughly and learned the most. One way they do this is to ask questions about confusing points of information. College professors know their course content very well and, therefore, they know the kinds of information that are likely to be "straight" in the minds of only the very best students in their classes.

You will understand this point better if you try to solve some problems. Read the following passages and decide which one contains information that is likely to confuse students:

1. A euphemism is a pleasant term for what may be a very unpleasant idea. Since the idea is unpleasant, the euphemism remains a euphemism only for a time and then it, too, becomes unpleasant, and a new euphemism is needed.

   Note the names for women's sizes: junior, misses, women's half-sizes, petites. Women's blouses are sized large, so that almost anyone can take size 12, 14, or 16, but skirts are smaller, so that most can take size 8, 10, or 12. Stretch stockings are not sized small, medium, large, and extra large, but short, average, long, and extra long. This pleases milady, for no woman wants to be considered extra large, but extra long is fine.*

2. We all have two types of vocabularies—*receptive* and *expressive*. Our receptive vocabulary is composed of the words we recognize through reading and listening. This vocabulary is usually several

---

* From Burmeister, READING STRATEGIES FOR SECONDARY SCHOOL TEACHERS, 1974, Addison-Wesley, Reading, Mass.

times larger than our expressive vocabulary, which is made up of the words we use when we speak and write. Our total vocabulary is composed of the words we recognize and/or use in receptive and expressive ways.*

I have tested hundreds of students on the information in these two passages and have found that most students are not confused about the meaning of *euphemism* but many students become confused over the differences between *expressive vocabulary* and *receptive vocabulary*. Some students cannot seem to remember that the expressive vocabulary contains words you use when you speak or write and that the receptive vocabulary contains words you know when you read or listen.

When you are confused over some point of information, this should be a signal to you to give the information special attention in your learning. If professors want to write test questions that will be answered correctly only by the students who have the most comprehensive knowledge, they will use confusing information as the basis for some of these questions.

METHOD THREE: PAY ATTENTION TO UNEXPECTED FACTS

The unexpected fact is closely related to confusing information. College professors can find challenging test items for students simply by writing questions about information that is contrary to expectations. For some reason people have difficulty learning or understanding something that is contrary to what they believe or expect.

To understand this, use your common sense to select the best answers for the following questions. Try to answer these questions before you read the explanations that follow them:

1. A trademark is best said to be
   a. the name under which a company does business.
   b. the picture or symbol associated with a product.
   c. the person or figure that represents a product.
   d. the name by which people speak of a product.

2. Your car was damaged when a tree fell over on it and you were glad you had
   a. fire and theft insurance.
   b. collision insurance.
   c. public liability insurance.
   d. property-damage liability insurance.

3. When a friend died and left you $5,000, you were correct in saying that you received the money by
   a. inheritance.
   b. legacy.
   c. accession.
   d. remittance.

* From Burmeister, READING STRATEGIES FOR SECONDARY SCHOOL TEACHERS, 1974, Addison-Wesley, Reading, Mass.

4. All of the following are considered to be real property except
   a. land.
   b. air.
   c. weeds.
   d. rocks.
   e. ducks.

If you tried to use your common sense and had not learned any of this information before, you probably did very poorly in answering these questions because each one has an answer that is contrary to what might reasonably be expected. Here are the answers:

1. A *trademark* is the name by which a product is known. All products have names by which they are known, but not all have a picture or symbol associated with them.
2. If a tree fell on your car, you should have been glad you had *fire and theft insurance* because it covers damage done by flying objects.
3. You should have said that you received the $5,000 by *legacy*, not inheritance.
4. Land, air, weeds, and rocks are *real property*, but ducks are not.

In studying for your courses it is very easy to pass over or dismiss information that does not fit into your expectations. Therefore, as you study, be on the alert for information that is true but does not conform to the pattern of what you believe to be true. This kind of information can be used as the basis for first-class test items. Your professors often know the kinds of information students reject; and when they want to include some difficult test questions, they may use such information to write the questions.

METHOD FOUR:
PAY ATTENTION TO
THE APPARENTLY FAMILIAR

Another way for instructors to find test items that will be answered correctly only by the students who have studied most thoroughly is to ask questions about information that appears to be familiar. Such apparently familiar information is of two basic types: (1) information we think we know, but about which we cannot answer questions accurately, and (2) information that is so easy to understand that it seems like common sense. A good deal of what students need to learn in college falls into one of these categories.

Many times these types of information are overlooked during study because students mistakenly believe that if they think they know something or if something seems like common sense, they will be able to answer test questions about it without studying. This assumption often does not hold true; after all, it is one thing to think we know or understand something, but it is something entirely different to be able to answer test questions about it.

Earlier in this book you read about examples and illustrations. Even before you read this information, you probably thought that you knew what examples and illustrations were. Test yourself to see if you can write answers to the following questions without looking up the answers:

1. What is an *example?* _____

_____

_____

2. What is an *illustration?* _____

_____

_____

Example and *illustration* are words you have heard and used most of your life, but were you able to answer the questions accurately and completely? For the first question you should have written an answer that includes most of this information: "An example is something selected to show the general characteristics of a person, place, or thing." If your definition of *example* is complete, then it would have been enough to say, "An illustration is a long example."

The other kind of apparently familiar information is the kind that is so easy to understand that it seems like common sense. Specific information about "commonsense" matters, however, is often difficult to retain unless special effort is expended to learn it. The following two questions are based on information you studied earlier in this book. Try to answer them without looking back in the book for help.

1. Give two reasons why it is not a good idea to cram for tests.

a. _____

_____

_____

b. _____

_____

_____

2. List three situations in which it would be a good idea to study with somebody else when preparing for a test.

a. _____

_____

_____

b. _____

_____

_____

c. _____

_____

_____

How many times have you lost points on a test because you could not give the answers to simple questions like these? The answers are simple and sensible but also very difficult to give correctly unless you have studied to answer them. Give yourself full credit for the first question if you answered that (a) "most information is best learned over a long period of time rather than in a short time span," and (b) "it is difficult for students to learn when they are rushed, feeling guilty, and worried about how well they will do on a test." For the second question you should have written (a) "when you study with somebody who knows as much as you do," (b) "when you study with somebody who is teaching you," and (c) "when you feel so lonely you cannot study alone."

Students who take tests on information such as this often complain that such tests are unfair: they understand the information, they claim, but could not answer questions about it. However, there is nothing unfair about such questions; there is nothing unfair about testing students on information they understand! Therefore, especially when you are taught things you think you know or understand, you should anticipate test questions on them and prepare yourself to answer them.

OTHER APPLICATIONS OF THESE METHODS

The explanations in the preceding sections have been given to help you understand exactly how to use certain techniques to improve your performance on college tests, but these techniques apply equally to ensuring that you have mastered anything you want to master. In learning information for a course, you should observe what a professor does in the classroom; on a job, you would observe a person who is expert in an area in which you wish to become expert. Also, if you learn on a job what is confusing, contrary to expectations, and apparently already known, you will have learned everything there is to learn! Thus, the four ways to anticipate test questions are ways to verify that you have learned certain information thoroughly, and you may use them to check that you have mastered information in college courses, things you need to know on a job, or anything else you want to learn throughout your lifetime.

PRACTICING WITH ANTICIPATING TEST QUESTIONS

On the following pages you will find two forms you can use to practice the four methods for anticipating test questions. The forms are designed to be used in other college courses you are taking so you may understand how skills taught in this book are to be transferred to the study of your college courses.

Assignment 1

Anticipating Test Questions

Practice the four ways to anticipate test questions in another course you are taking. Write the name of the course, the teacher's name, and the title of the textbook you use in the course.

Course: _____

Teacher: _____

Textbook: _____

1. _Be observant in class._ Teachers are likely to ask test questions about important things they write on the chalkboard. The next time you go to this class, notice the important things your teacher writes on the chalkboard. Write some of them on the lines provided.

_____

_____

_____

_____

_____

Teachers are also likely to ask test questions about things they emphasize in class (especially if these things are not emphasized in the textbook). The next time you go to this class, notice the things your teacher emphasizes. Write some of them on the lines provided.

_____

_____

_____

_____

_____

2. _Pay attention to confusing information._ Teachers are likely to ask test questions about confusing information. The next time you read your

(continued)

textbook for this course, make a note about a piece of information that would be confusing to learn. Write it on the lines provided.

_____

_____

_____

_____

_____

_____

3. *Pay attention to unexpected facts.* Teachers are likely to ask test questions about facts that are different from, or contrary to, what might be expected. The next time you read your textbook for this course, make a note about a fact that is different from what you previously believed the facts to be. Write it on the lines provided.

_____

_____

_____

_____

_____

_____

4. *Pay attention to the apparently familiar.* Teachers are likely to ask test questions about things that are easy to understand, but difficult to remember unless they are studied. The next time you read your textbook for this course, make a note about information that is easy to understand, but that you would need to study in preparation for a test. Write it on the lines provided.

_____

_____

_____

_____

_____

Assignment 2

Anticipating Test Questions

Select a course other than the one you selected when you did Assignment 1 for this lesson. Write the name of the other course, the other teacher, and the other textbook.

Course: _____

Teacher: _____

Textbook: _____

1. *Be observant in class*. Teachers are likely to ask test questions about important things they write on the chalkboard. The next time you go to this class, notice the important things your teacher writes on the chalkboard. Write some of them on the lines provided.

_____

_____

_____

_____

_____

_____

Teachers are also likely to ask test questions about things they emphasize in class (especially if these things are not emphasized in the textbook). The next time you go to this class, notice the things your teacher emphasizes. Write some of them on the lines provided.

_____

_____

_____

_____

_____

_____

2. *Pay attention to confusing information*. Teachers are likely to ask test questions about confusing information. The next time you read your

(continued)

textbook for this course, make a note about a piece of information that would be confusing to learn. Write it on the lines provided.

_____

_____

_____

_____

_____

3. *Pay attention to unexpected facts.* Teachers are likely to ask test questions about facts that are different from, or contrary to, what might be expected. The next time you read your textbook for this course, make a note about a fact that is different from what you previously believed the facts to be. Write it on the lines provided.

_____

_____

_____

_____

_____

4. *Pay attention to the apparently familiar.* Teachers are likely to ask test questions about things that are easy to understand, but difficult to remember unless they are studied. The next time you read your textbook for this course, make a note about information that is easy to understand, but that you would need to study in preparation for a test. Write it on the lines provided.

_____

_____

_____

_____

_____

Lesson 12. Anticipating the Unexpected

High school tests are likely to have questions that require students to give information in answers in the same way the information was learned. For example, if high school students in an English course learned the meanings of the words *simile, metaphor,* and *personification,* a high school teacher is likely to test students by asking them to give the meanings of these words.

However, in college, students find their understanding is often tested in ways that are different from the ways in which they studied. For example, college students may have learned about personification by memorizing its meaning, but in a test they might find that they are asked to do something other than give its meaning. They may be asked to give an example of personification, or to explain how personification is different from metaphor. Most students are surprised when this happens but are able to overcome their momentary disorientation and go on to answer questions correctly. Others become so confused that they cannot answer questions even though they have the information needed to answer them. Also, if many questions on a test require students to show their understanding by doing something other than that for which they specifically studied, a good number of students will do more poorly on the test than they should have done.

The fact is that you should always *anticipate the unexpected on tests in college.* There are so many ways in which your knowledge of information can be tested that it would be almost impossible for you to prepare yourself for every possibility. You will be more relaxed when taking tests if you are prepared for the test questions not to be exactly what you expect.

**FOUR TYPES
OF TEST QUESTIONS**

Most college tests will measure, at least to some degree, your understanding of terminology that is important to the courses you are studying. When this is the case, there are four basic forms questions might take:

Type 1. A term is given and you are asked to give its definition.

Type 2. A term is given and you are asked to provide an example.

Type 3. A definition is given and you are asked what term it defines.

Type 4. An example is given and you are asked to give the term for which it is an example.

A sample of each of these four types of questions follows. These sample questions are written in the multiple-choice format and test a student's knowledge of the meaning of the term *personification.* Please study the questions carefully.

TYPE 1: TERM GIVEN, YOU GIVE DEFINITION

Personification is the technique of
a. representing a thing or animal as a person.
b. comparing two things using *like* or *as*.
c. using a pleasant term for an unpleasant idea.
d. using overstatement to express a thought.

TYPE 2: TERM GIVEN, YOU GIVE EXAMPLE

Which of the following is *not* an example of personification?
a. The old house told a strange story.
b. The alarm clock woke me up today.
c. My dog ordered Alpo for dinner.
d. This land is your dear mother.

TYPE 3: DEFINITION GIVEN, YOU GIVE TERM

When writers represent a thing or animal as a person, they use
the technique of
a. personification.
b. denotation.
c. euphemism.
d. narration.

TYPE 4: EXAMPLE GIVEN, YOU GIVE TERM

"The sun smiled down on us" is an example of
a. euphemism.
b. metaphor.
c. exposition.
d. personification.

PRACTICE WITH FOUR TYPES OF TEST QUESTIONS

The problems for this lesson will help you understand how your knowledge of information may be tested in different ways. The problems are test questions based on the textbook passages on pages 52–62, and each question is either a Type 1, Type 2, Type 3, or Type 4 question. You solve the problems (1) by deciding if the question gives you a term, a definition, or an example; (2) by deciding if you must answer with a term, a definition, or an example; and (3) by giving the answer for the question. The first problem is solved for you so you will understand what you are to do.

Class Practice

Studying Test Questions

These problems are based on passages 1-10, which are on pages 52-56. The first problem has been done for you.

1. "She is as pretty as a picture" is a(n) _____ .

You are given: term   definition   (example)

You must give: (term)   definition   example

Answer: _Simile_ _____

2. Give the meaning of *metaphor*.

You are given: term   definition   example

You must give: term   definition   example

Answer: _____

3. Give an example of a personification.

You are given: term   definition   example

You must give: term   definition   example

Answer: _____

4. To refer to someone as a *senior citizen* rather than an *old person* is to use a(n) _____ .

You are given: term   definition   example

You must give: term   definition   example

Answer: _____

5. Words known when read or heard are words in the _____ vocabulary.

You are given: term   definition   example

You must give: term   definition   example

Answer: _____

6. Write a sentence in which the word *heart* is used with a denotative meaning.

You are given: term   definition   example

You must give: term   definition   example

Answer: _____

7. "The mayor is under fire." In what sense is the word *fire* used in this sentence?

You are given: term   definition   example

You must give: term   definition   example

Answer: _____

8. Something selected to show the general characteristics of a person, place, or thing is called a(n) _____ .

You are given: term   definition   example

You must give: term   definition   example

Answer: _____

9. Explain how illustrations are different from instances.

You are given: term   definition   example

You must give: term   definition   example

Answer: _____

10. Give an example of a literal analogy.

You are given: term   definition   example

You must give: term   definition   example

Answer: _____

Assignment 1

Studying Test Questions

These problems are based on passages 11-20 on pages 56-60.

1. If a friend told you a story about something that happened on his vacation, he would need to use _____ .

   You are given: term   definition   example

   You must give: term   definition   example

Answer: _____

2. Most information in cookbooks takes the form of _____ .

   You are given: term   definition   example

   You must give: term   definition   example

Answer: _____

3. List four kinds of personal property.

   You are given: term   definition   example

   You must give: term   definition   example

Answer: _____

4. Phil ran his car into a fence on the way to school. The damage to the fence will be paid for by Phil's _____ insurance.

   You are given: term   definition   example

   You must give: term   definition   example

Answer: _____

5. Property acquired by means of a will is property acquired by _____ .

   You are given: term   definition   example

   You must give: term   definition   example

Answer: _____

(continued)

6. A person who takes another person to court is called the
_____ .

You are given:	term	definition	example
You must give:	term	definition	example

Answer: _____

7. Under what conditions may a baby be classified as being premature?

You are given:	term	definition	example
You must give:	term	definition	example

Answer: _____

8. _____ are repeated physical movements that are symptomatic of psychological tension, repressed needs, or repressed conflicts.

You are given:	term	definition	example
You must give:	term	definition	example

Answer: _____

9. Give an example of sex-typing.

You are given:	term	definition	example
You must give:	term	definition	example

Answer: _____

10. Mary says she loves John, but I've never seen her as angry at anybody as she is at John right now. Mary must have a(n) _____ toward John.

You are given:	term	definition	example
You must give:	term	definition	example

Answer: _____

Assignment 2

Studying Test Questions

These problems are based on passages 21–30 on pages 60–62.

1. Give an example of frustration.

    You are given:　　　term　　　definition　　　example

    You must give:　　　term　　　definition　　　example

Answer: _____

2. The extreme motive to inflict pain on oneself is called _____ .

    You are given:　　　term　　　definition　　　example

    You must give:　　　term　　　definition　　　example

Answer: _____

3. Mrs. Twerp screamed her head off when the check-out person over-charged her for butter. Mrs. Twerp exhibited _____ .

    You are given:　　　term　　　definition　　　example

    You must give:　　　term　　　definition　　　example

Answer: _____

4. What do anthropologists, sociologists, and psychologists study?

    You are given:　　　term　　　definition　　　example

    You must give:　　　term　　　definition　　　example

Answer: _____

5. All advertising that is to be printed in the July issue of a particular magazine must be in the hands of the publisher by June 5. June 5 is an example of a(n) _____ date.

    You are given:　　　term　　　definition　　　example

    You must give:　　　term　　　definition　　　example

Answer: _____

(*continued*)

6. People who buy a magazine by subscription or on a newsstand are part of the magazine's _____ circulation.

    You are given: term   definition   example

    You must give: term   definition   example

Answer: _____

7. _____ are the names by which products are known.

    You are given: term   definition   example

    You must give: term   definition   example

Answer: _____

8. Advertising that requests people to respond with their name and address is called _____ advertising.

    You are given: term   definition   example

    You must give: term   definition   example

Answer: _____

9. Give an example of how somebody might participate in mail-order advertising.

    You are given: term   definition   example

    You must give: term   definition   example

Answer: _____

10. Describe a way in which direct-mail advertising has affected you.

    You are given: term   definition   example

    You must give: term   definition   example

Answer: _____

Lesson 13. Reciting and Reviewing

Reciting is the act of repeating information to yourself so it can be remembered and recalled. For example, if you have read about *sex-typing* in a psychology textbook, you might decide that your instructor will ask you a question about sex-typing on a test. In reciting you would ask yourself, "What is sex-typing?" and give the answer to your question without looking at the answer in your notes. *Reviewing* is the repetition of recitation until information has been completely learned.

RECITING

In Lesson 6 it was very strongly stated that *reciting is believed to be the single most important step in any study program.* The reasons given for this were:

1. When students recite information, they are more likely to remember and recall it than if they simply read and reread it.
2. Reciting forces learners to select the things they want to learn.
3. Reciting prepares students for the test-taking situation because it is very much like taking a test. When students take tests, they give the answers to questions; when they recite, they also give answers to questions.

Reciting from Textbooks. Some students attempt to study for tests by reciting from their marked textbooks. They use their markings to locate quickly the things they want to learn, look away from the book, recite the important information, and then check in the book to make certain they recited the information accurately. The success of this method is difficult to determine, but there are at least two major problems with trying to recite from textbooks:

1. Information that is not learned during the first recitation may be overlooked in the textbook and never learned.
2. If a textbook presentation is confusing, students may attempt to learn information in words that they do not completely understand.

Experienced students, then, recite instead from written notes, because they can isolate the things they want to learn and can study information recorded in their own words.

Reciting from Textbook Notes. In Lesson 9 it was illustrated how a student made a study card to learn about transfer of learning. This study card is repeated in Figure 13.1. The information could have been put into study notes as well as onto a study card; but whatever the type of notes made, the same procedure may be used for recitation.

Figure 13.1   An Example of a Study Card That Could Be Used to Recite Information About Transfer of Learning

Back of study card for ''transfer of learning''

> The influence learning one thing has on learning something else.
>
> 1. Positive transfer is the process by which learning one thing helps learning other things. (Learning to drive a car helps learning to drive a truck.)
>
> 2. Negative transfer is the process by which learning one thing does not help learning other things. (Learning to drive on the right side of the road makes it difficult to drive on the left side of the road when visiting England.)

A student would probably learn the information in the sample study card in Figure 13.1 most efficiently by reading ''transfer of learning'' from the front of the card and then reciting in this way:

1. ''Transfer of learning is the influence learning one thing has on learning something else.''
2. ''There are two types of transfer of learning: positive and negative.''
3. ''Positive transfer is the process by which learning one thing helps in learning other things. For example, learning to type on one typewriter should help me learn to type on other typewriters.''
4. ''Negative transfer is the process by which learning one thing does *not* help in learning other things. For example, if I get fat because I've learned to eat something sweet with every meal, it will be difficult for me to get thin by learning not to eat sweet things all the time.''

Two things are important about this example of recitation. *First,* the two types of transfer (positive and negative) are recited before their definitions are recited. This helps in learning the outline on the card. *Second,* the examples given during recitation are not the same as those on the card. When different examples are given for positive and negative transfer, it becomes clear that the concepts are really understood—and that recitation is more than the simple rote memorization of words.

Reciting from Lecture Notes. The procedures used for reciting from textbook notes may also be applied to studying the information in lecture notes. In courses in which professors lecture, it is almost always important to give careful attention to learning the material covered in lectures. You should use one or more of the following suggestions to help you learn information in lecture notes:

1. When you make your lecture notes, leave a wide margin on the lefthand side of the page. Read through your notes and decide what questions might be asked about them. Write the questions in the appropriate places in the margins and use your questions for recitation and review. For example, if information in your lecture notes explains three ways in which property may be acquired, you might write "What are three ways property may be acquired?" in the wide lefthand margin. You would use this question as the basis for recitation.
2. Read through your notes and mark the headings or major thoughts so they stand out clearly. (Some students use a yellow highlight pen for this purpose.) Use the information marked in yellow as the basis for recitation, just as you would use the items recorded on the front of your study cards.
3. If you make study cards for your textbooks, put information from your lecture notes on study cards also. Integrate the cards from the textbook with the cards from the lecture notes. For example, if you have a textbook card on *sex-typing* for a psychology course, write the information about sex-typing that was given in the lecture on this card; make a second card if there is not room for this information on the first one. In this way you can learn all the information about sex-typing at one time instead of learning information from the textbook and the lectures separately. This use of study cards is an extremely efficient way to study for tests in lecture courses.

Using Mnemonic Devices in Recitation. Sometimes it is helpful to construct a mnemonic device to aid the process of recall. The device may be written on the front of study cards or in the lefthand column of study notes. One student learned the three ways in which property may be acquired by using the mnemonic acronym *AIL: A* recalled *accession, I* recalled *inheritance,* and *L* recalled *legacy.* The student recited in this way:

1. "There are three ways in which property may be acquired (AIL): accession, inheritance, and legacy."
2. "Accession is getting property by an increase in something owned, as when dogs have puppies."
3. "Inheritance is getting property because of inheritance laws."
4. "Legacy is getting property by means of a will."

Again, the list of things to be learned was recited before the details about each term were recited. The student recited an example only for accession because this item is the one best understood by use of an example. The advantages and disadvantages of mnemonic devices are discussed in Lesson 5.

Using Study Cards in Recitation. Most students make their notes for study on pieces of paper, not on 3 × 5 index cards. However, study cards are so useful that their advantages are repeated here to give you one more opportunity to consider using them:

1. In Lesson 9 it was stated that study cards make it easy to separate the things you know from those you do not know. Thus, you can spend your study time learning the things you do not know instead of constantly going over things you have already learned.
2. In this lesson it was explained how study cards can be used to integrate textbook information with lecture information so you can learn everything about a topic simultaneously instead of at different times.

These advantages are both important aids to efficient learning, which cannot be achieved as easily in any other way as with the use of study cards.

What to Do When You Fail to Learn. There will be times when you will experience difficulty learning some information no matter how much you recite. If you survey, mark your textbooks, make written notes, recite, and still do not learn the information you want to learn, you should try doing one of these things:

1. *Recite by writing answers on paper rather than by saying them to yourself.* In mathematics courses you recite when you write solutions to problems you want to learn to solve; in foreign language courses you recite by writing the language you want to learn. Just as writing helps you learn in mathematics and foreign language courses, it can also help you learn in those situations in which oral recitation fails you.
2. *Construct a mnemonic acronym or mnemonic sentence as described in Lesson 5.*
3. *Put the information you are having difficulty learning into a classification chart if it is logical to do so.* In Lesson 22 you will learn about classification charts, which may be used to learn information that tells how two or more persons, places, or things are alike or different in two or more ways. If information you have difficulty learning fits this description, it is easier to study when it is put in the classification chart format presented in Lesson 22.

Except for the four steps in the SOAR study formula, the preceding list is the most important list in this book. When the SOAR study formula is insufficient for learning, one of these three suggestions is likely to help you. Study the suggestions carefully and refer to them whenever you have difficulty learning.

REVIEWING

Reviewing is simply repeating recitation until all the information has been learned as completely as possible. It is included with reciting to help you understand that you should not expect to be able to learn all the information you want to learn by reciting it only once or twice. Reciting and reviewing are the essential ingredients in an effective study program; they make it possible for you to learn information thoroughly so you can remember and recall it when you are tested on it.

PRACTICE WITH RECITING

If you are taking other college courses, the value of reciting can be appreciated fully if you use study notes or study cards to recite for tests in your courses. If you followed the suggestion in Lesson 9 and made study cards or study notes for another college course, use those notes to recite for a test you will take in the other course. Also, if you followed the suggestion in Lesson 9 and made study cards or study notes to study for any of the five tests listed on page 70, use the notes you made to prepare for the tests.

Practice reciting with a friend, relative, or fellow student. After you have made your notes, have somebody test you on how well you know the information in them. You may find it particularly helpful to practice with a student who is learning the same information you are learning, since you can test each other and learn together.

Part 3. Developing Organizational Skills

In Part 2 you practiced marking books and making notes for textbook passages that explain the meanings of important words. Although it is valuable to have an efficient way to learn the new terms you will need to know in your college courses, textbooks contain many kinds of information other than the meanings of terminology. The purpose of this part of the book is to help you develop your organizational skills so that you will become more expert at marking and making notes on *any* information in your textbooks. This purpose is achieved by teaching you how to make outlines. In Part 3 are six lessons for learning about outlines and three lessons for using organizational skills. These lessons are grouped as shown at the left.

Some students feel that Lessons 20, 21, and 22, on using organizational skills, are the important lessons in this part of the book and that Lessons 14 through 19, on learning to make outlines, are unnecessary. However, Lesson 14 through 19 have been carefully developed over a long period of time to ensure that most college students who study them will learn to make good outlines. The only students who should not study Lesson 14 through 19 are those who can already make good outlines for the practice passages in Lesson 20. No matter how easy or difficult an exercise may seem, you will improve your organizational skills more quickly if you do your best to work out carefully all the exercises in the order in which they are given.

Lesson 14. Introduction to Outlines

You have learned in writing courses that sentences and paragraphs have certain characteristics. For example, you have learned that paragraphs are indented, that they contain a statement of a major thought, and that all the additional information they contain is related to the major thought. Outlines also have their own characteristics.

**CHARACTERISTICS
OF OUTLINES**

Outlines are written summaries in which Roman numerals are placed in front of major thoughts, capital letters are placed in front of details, and Arabic numerals are placed in front of minor details. The following is an example of an outline:

> OUTLINES
>
> I. A good outline passes two tests.
>   A. It is an accurate summary of information.
>   B. It is well organized to show how ideas are related.
> II. Outlines must be in the correct format.
>   A. They begin with a title.
>   B. Their statements are correctly labeled.
>   1. Roman numerals label major thoughts.
>   2. Capital letters label details.
>   3. Arabic numerals label minor details.

You may understand the importance of learning to write paragraphs but be uncertain about the importance of making outlines. On page 64 of this book is a passage from a psychology textbook that explains the principle of transfer of learning. *Transfer of learning* is the influence that the learning of one task has on the learning of other tasks. For example, if you learn to write good essays in a writing class, you should be able to transfer what you learn to writing term papers, letters, or anything else. Making outlines requires that you find major thoughts and details and show the relationships among them in a particularly exacting way. If you learn to make outlines, you will learn skills that have excellent *positive transfer* to doing these things:

1. reading and understanding textbooks
2. marking textbooks accurately
3. making notes from textbooks
4. making good lecture notes

As you study outlining, you must recognize that you are learning to make outlines for the purpose of learning organizational skills, which have positive transfer of learning to studying. You are not simply going to learn to make lecture notes or textbook notes in the outline format, but rather you are going to develop your outlining skills *so that* you will make better lecture and textbook notes no matter what format you use.

MAJOR THOUGHTS IN OUTLINES

The basic problem in making outlines is to determine what the major thoughts are so that details may be listed under them correctly. When a major thought is a word, it is a word that may be used to identify a group of persons, places, or things. For example, in this outline *North America* and *Europe* are the major thoughts used to identify groups of places:

COUNTRIES

   I. North America
      A. United States
      B. Canada
      C. Mexico
  II. Europe
      A. Italy
      B. France
      C. Germany

PRACTICE WITH FINDING MAJOR THOUGHTS

There are two types of exercises for identifying major thoughts, when major thoughts are words. In one type, the major thoughts are mixed in with other words in a list. You solve a problem by reading the list and circling the major thoughts. The major thoughts are circled in this sample list. (The arrows show that you are to read all the way down one column before going on to the next.)

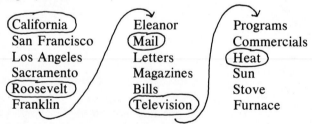

In the second type of exercise you are given a list of four things, and you write a major thought for each list. Write a major thought for this sample list:

_____

Penny
Nickel
Dime
Quarter

Several major thoughts are possible choices, but *coins* is probably the best. *Money* is another possibility, but it is not as good as *coins* because all this money is coins.

Class Practice

Major Thoughts

Circle the major thoughts in the list. The first major thought is *Kitchen*.

Kitchen	Theater	Pear	-er
Stove	Character	Shape	Writer
Refrigerator	Honest	Square	Shakespeare
Blender	Lazy	Round	Wordsworth
Dishwasher	Tactful	Triangle	Longfellow
Emotion	Thoughtful	Oblong	Country
Hate	Argumentative	Oval	France
Envy	Agreeable	Cone	Italy
Fear	Writing	Prefix	Japan
Love	Letter	Mis-	Iraq
Against	Newspaper	Dis-	River
Antiwar	Magazine	Contra-	Nile
Antilabor	Weekday	Anti-	Columbia
Antislavery	Monday	Time	Mississippi
Favoring	Tuesday	Second	Congo
Prowar	Wednesday	Minute	Amazon
Prolabor	Thursday	Hour	Rhine
Proslavery	Month	Nut	Beverage
Store	May	Walnut	Milk
Grocery	June	Almond	Coffee
Bakery	July	Cashew	Tea
Drugstore	August	Vegetable	Meat
Disaster	March	Potato	Beef
Flood	Women	Lettuce	Lamb
Fire	May	Carrot	Pork
Famine	June	Cabbage	Fowl
Disease	Christine	Asparagus	Chicken
Measles	Dog	Bread	Turkey
Colds	Collie	Rolls	Duck
Mumps	Spaniel	Buns	Quail
Chicken pox	Terrier	Biscuits	Singer
Entertainment	Fruit	Suffix	Popular
Television	Banana	-less	Classical
Movies	Apple	-tion	Western

Write a major thought for each list.

1. _____	**2.** _____
Red	Hat
Yellow	Shoes
Green	Shirt
Orange	Pants

3.* _____

Whippet
Dingo
Griffon
Mastiff

4.* _____

Acute
Oblique
Reflex
Salient

5. _____

Sewing
Cleaning
Washing
Cooking

6. _____

Cheddar
Swiss
American
Cream

7. _____

January
February
September
November

8. _____

Man
Girl
Boy
Woman

9. _____

Breakfast
Lunch
Dinner
Supper

10. _____

Shark
Salmon
Trout
Pike

11.* _____

Garnet
Pumice
Rasp
Emery

12. _____

Ballet
Sculpture
Painting
Opera

* Included to demonstrate why familiar words must be used in these lists.

Assignment

Major Thoughts

Circle the major thoughts in the list. The first major thought is *Clothes*.

Clothes	Paper	Hydrogen	Animal
Hat	Envelope	Fish	Cow
Shoes	Literature	Tuna	Horse
Coat	Novel	Salmon	Pig
Pants	Poem	Shark	Sheep
Shirt	Drama	Sport	Kangaroo
Game	Instrument	Skating	Insect
Ping-Pong	Violin	Swimming	Spider
Marbles	Trumpet	Fishing	Cockroach
Ocean	Saxophone	Hiking	Caterpillar
Atlantic	Cello	Surfing	Bird
Pacific	Oboe	Stone	Robin
Island	Bass	Diamond	Seagull
Hawaii	Fish	Ruby	Sparrow
Puerto Rico	Bass	Flower	Pigeon
Cuba	Sardine	Rose	Tree
Tool	Flounder	Lily	Oak
Hammer	Carp	Carnation	Birch
Screwdriver	Painter	Lilac	Willow
Wrench	Picasso	Gardenia	Magazine
Face	Van Gogh	Tulip	*Time*
Eyebrow	Rembrandt	Mathematics	*Newsweek*
Lips	Snake	Algebra	*Playboy*
Nose	Rattler	Trigonometry	Fabric
Eyelash	Cobra	Calculus	Cotton
Cheek	Python	Language	Wool
Chin	Viper	French	Nylon
Weapon	Furniture	German	Rayon
Gun	Sofa	Spanish	Orlon
Rifle	Chair	English	Measure
Bomb	Table	City	Inch
Cannon	Dresser	Seattle	Foot
Knife	Bomb	Cincinnati	Yard
Stationery	Atomic	Denver	Mile

Write a major thought for each list

1. _____

Lettuce
Potatoes
Cabbage
Beans

2. _____

Cake
Pie
Ice cream
Pudding

(*continued*)

3. _____

Car
Airplane
Train
Bus

4. _____

Arizona
Wisconsin
California
Texas

5. _____

Helicopter
Glider
Jet
Balloon

6. _____

Truman
Kennedy
Johnson
Carter

7. _____

Easter
Christmas
Thanksgiving
Labor Day

8. _____

Helen
Bob
Mary
Jim

9. _____

Rose
Orchid
Carnation
Tulip

10. _____

Chevrolet
Pontiac
Ford
Plymouth

11. _____

Steam
Atomic
Electric
Gasoline

12. _____

Europe
Asia
Africa
South America

Lesson 15. Labeling Major Thoughts and Details

In this lesson you will learn to label outlines with Roman numerals for major thoughts and with capital letters for details. The logic of this labeling system is important to understand.

THE LOGIC OF OUTLINES

There are two ways to understand the *logic* of outlines. The first is to examine the relations among ideas directly from an outline by marking the outline as shown in Figure 15.1. *Box 1,* which joins the Roman numerals (major thoughts) to the title, indicates that the major thoughts are checked against the title. The use of Roman numerals to label North America and Europe is logical because both are continents that contain some countries. *Box 2* and *Box 3* indicate that capital letters (details) are checked against Roman numerals (major thoughts). The labeling of United States, Canada, and Mexico with capital letters in Box 2 is logical because the three are countries in North America. Likewise, the labeling of Italy and France with capital letters in Box 3 is logical because both are European countries.

The second way to check and understand the logic of outlines is to put outlines into a diagram such as the one in Figure 15.2. The boxes over the diagram in Figure 15.2 show that the logic is checked in the same way used

Figure 15.1   An Outline That Is Marked to Show How to Check the Logic of an Outline Containing Major Thoughts and Details

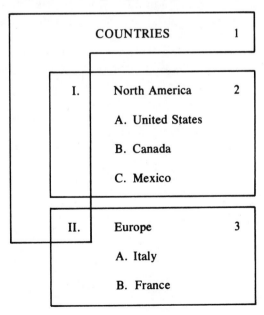

COUNTRIES   1

I.   North America   2

       A. United States

       B. Canada

       C. Mexico

II.   Europe   3

       A. Italy

       B. France

Figure 15.2   A Diagram of an Outline That Is Marked to Show How to Check the Logic of an Outline Containing Major Thoughts and Details

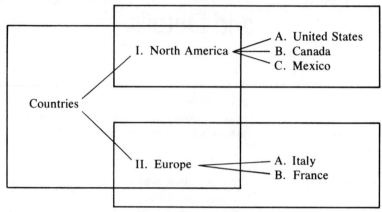

in Figure 15.1: Major thoughts (labeled with Roman numerals) are checked against the title, and details (labeled with capital letters) are checked against major thoughts. Keep these procedures in mind as you solve all the problems in this part of the book.

PRACTICE WITH LABELING MAJOR THOUGHTS AND DETAILS

The problems for this lesson will help you to understand how ideas are related and to learn the numbering and lettering system used to label major thoughts and details in the outline format. The problems may seem unnecessarily easy, but practice in doing them will help you do more easily the increasingly difficult problems in following lessons. Use these directions to solve the problems:

1. Read a list to find the words that seem to divide the list. These are the major thoughts. Number them with Roman numerals in the first column of the grid.
2. The other words in the list are details. Letter them with capital letters in the second column of the grid. Begin with the letter A under each Roman numeral.
3. Write a title for the list.

A sample problem has been solved for you to show you how the exercises are done. Be certain that you understand the sample before going on to solve the other problems.

Class Practice

Major Thoughts and Details

Some Countries

I.		North America
	A.	United States
	B.	Canada
	C.	Mexico
II.		Europe
	A.	Italy
	B.	France
	C.	Germany
	D.	Switzerland

1.

		Asia
		India
		China
		Africa
		Morocco
		Egypt
		South America
		Brazil
		Argentina

2.

		Blade
		Sword
		Knife
		Rapier
		Bomb
		Atomic
		Hydrogen
		Rifle
		Hunting
		Combat

3.

		Bird
		Cuckoo
		Gull
		Dog
		Greyhound
		Terrier
		Spaniel
		Poodle
		Snake
		Asp
		Python
		Boa

4.

		Red
		Cherry
		Carnation
		Lobster
		Green
		Pea
		Moss
		Olive
		Purple
		Lilac
		Plum

5.

		Length
		Yard
		Foot
		Inch
		Mile
		Volume
		Gallon
		Quart
		Pint
		Cup
		Ounce
		Weight
		Ton
		Pound
		Ounce

Assignment 1

Major Thoughts and Details

1.

		Produce
		Lettuce
		Apples
		Potatoes
		Carrots
		Onions
		Dairy
		Eggs
		Milk
		Cheese
		Yogurt
		Meat
		Hamburger
		Bacon
		Cleaning
		Window cleaner
		Scouring pads

2.

		Individual
		Hiking
		Swimming
		Bicycling
		Jogging
		Two-person
		Tennis
		Ping-Pong
		Badminton
		Team
		Football
		Baseball
		Soccer
		Basketball
		Volleyball
		Hockey

(*continued*)

3.

		Literature
		Novels
		Poetry
		Reference
		Dictionaries
		Encyclopedias
		Music
		Sheet music
		Recordings
		Music books
		Art
		Art books
		Prints of artwork
		Science
		Chemistry books
		Biology books
		Physics books

4.

		String
		Violin
		Viola
		Cello
		Bass
		Woodwind
		Flute
		Clarinet
		Bassoon
		Saxophone
		Brass
		Trumpet
		Trombone
		Tuba
		Percussion
		Xylophone
		Triangle
		Bass drum

Assignment 2

Major Thoughts and Details

1.

		Prefix
		Un-
		Dis-
		Mis-
		Anti-
		Suffix
		-er
		-less
		-ing
		-ment
		Root word
		Happy
		Count
		Peace
		Walk
		Derivative
		Unhappy
		Counter
		Peaceful

2.

		Sex
		Male
		Female
		Marital status
		Single
		Married
		Divorced
		Age
		Weight
		Height
		Address
		Street
		City
		State
		Zip code
		Education
		Grade school
		High school
		College
		Previous jobs

(*continued*)

3.

		Office
		Secretary
		Typist
		Clerk
		Manager
		Hospital
		Nurse
		Doctor
		Dietician
		School
		Teacher
		Principal
		Factory
		Store
		Buyer
		Sales clerk
		Wrapper

4.

		California
		San Francisco
		Los Angeles
		Monterey
		North Dakota
		Texas
		Houston
		Dallas
		Georgia
		Atlanta
		Savannah
		Macon
		New Jersey
		New Mexico
		Taos
		Albuquerque
		Santa Fe
		Oregon
		Massachusetts
		Boston
		Concord

Lesson 16. Coordination

In Lesson 17 you are going to learn to label minor details in outlines, and this is much more easily done when the concept of coordination is understood.

THE CONCEPT OF COORDINATION

The traditional outline system requires outlines to pass two tests: the *test of subordination* and the *test of coordination*. These abstract concepts are perhaps best understood by an example. The following outline passes the test of subordination, but does not pass the test of coordination. A discussion of why the outline passes one test, but not the other, directly follows its presentation. However, you may already understand something about coordination. Before you read the discussion about subordination and coordination, test your knowledge of coordination by crossing out any words in the following outline that are not coordinate.

FREQUENTLY VISITED PLACES

    I. North America
        A. United States
        B. Canada
        C. New York City
    II. Europe
        A. Italy
        B. The Alps
        C. France
    III. National parks
    IV. Asia
        A. China

The Test of Subordination. The outline passes the test of subordination for the following reasons:

1. The information labeled with Roman numerals is correctly related to the title: North America, Europe, national parks, and Asia are "frequently visited places."
2. The information labeled with capital letters is correctly related to Roman numerals: the United States, Canada, and New York City are in North America (I); Italy, the Alps, and France are in Europe (II); China is in Asia (IV).

The Test of Coordination. The items that have been crossed out in the outline where it is repeated below do not pass the test of coordination:

FREQUENTLY VISITED PLACES

  I. North America
     A. United States
     B. Canada
     ~~C. New York City~~
 II. Europe
     A. Italy
     ~~B. The Alps~~
     C. France
~~III. National parks~~
 IV. Asia
     ~~A. China~~

1. "National parks" is not coordinate with the information designated by the other Roman numerals because the parks do not constitute a continent. North America, Europe, and Asia are continents. "National parks" should be crossed out.
2. Under Roman numeral I, "New York City" is not coordinate with the information designated by the other capital letters because it is not a country. The United States and Canada are countries. "New York City" should be crossed out.
3. Under Roman numeral II, "The Alps" is not coordinate with the information designated by the other capital letters because the Alps are not a country. Italy and France are countries. "The Alps" should be crossed out.
4. Under Roman numeral IV, "China" is not coordinate with any other information because no other information is listed. There can be no coordination with only one item in a list. "China" should be crossed out.

IS COORDINATION NECESSARY?

Some authorities on outlining object to the requirement that outlines pass the test of coordination. One argument advanced is that since some writers do not use coordination when they write, it is not possible to use coordination when putting their material into an outline. This problem is illustrated in the following accurate outline of a short passage:

TYPES OF PLAYS WRITTEN BY SHAKESPEARE

  I. Comedies
     A. *Much Ado about Nothing*
     B. *Twelfth Night*
     C. *Comedy of Errors*
 II. Tragedies
     A. *Hamlet*
     B. *Macbeth*
III. Histories
     A. *Richard III*

Some experts would argue that it is correct to list *Richard III* next to an A with no B, because this style gives an accurate representation of the writer's organization of ideas. Such an argument is logical.

However, the important thing to remember is that, with all its faults, the coordinate outline system is widely used in the Western world. The materials in this book have been designed so you can learn the outline format in the way it is traditionally used; the problems in this book have *all* been written so you can observe the test of coordination. When you do the outlining problems in this book, you will *always* be able to observe coordination and you will have more accurate solutions to problems if you carefully consider coordination. Coordination has been included to help you know exactly what you are to do in this book so you can learn to outline more quickly.

Therefore, when you do any outlining problem in this book, you can be certain that

1. you should always use at least two Roman numerals (I and II);
2. if you use capital letters under a Roman numeral, you should always use at least two (A and B); and
3. if you use Arabic numerals under a capital letter, you should always use at least two (1 and 2).

This guide will help you learn to make good outlines. If you make an outline that has an A, but no B, under a Roman numeral, you will know you have made an error. Also, if you make an outline that has a 1, but no 2, under a capital letter, you will know you have done something incorrectly. Knowing you have made an error will often help you find a better solution.

WHAT NEEDS TO BE COORDINATE?

Some students are confused about outlines with the characteristics of this one:

CALIFORNIA AND WASHINGTON

    I. California
       A. San Francisco
       B. Los Angeles
   II. Washington
       A. Sailing
       B. Fishing
       C. Hunting

The confusion arises from the listing of cities under "California" and the subsequent listing of sporting activities under "Washington." One might assume that both listings should be from the same category, but this is not true. This outline could be for a speech about a trip to the states of California and Washington. While in California, the speaker might have visited San Francisco and Los Angeles but engaged in no outdoor activity. On the other hand, the interesting things about the visit to Washington might have been the sailing, fishing, and hunting. The general principle is:

There must be coordination within a subordinate listing in an outline, but there need not be coordination between or among subordinate listings in an outline.

In other words:

1. The information next to a series of capital letters must be coordinate, but it need not be coordinate with information next to other series of capital letters.
2. The information next to a series of Arabic numerals must be coordinate, but it need not be coordinate with information next to other series of Arabic numerals.

PRACTICE WITH RECOGNIZING COORDINATION

Do the following coordination problems in the same way you did the sample problem at the beginning of this lesson. The purpose of the coordination problems is to give you an opportunity to think about the importance of coordination. When you discuss the solutions to the problems, members of your class will come to different conclusions about what should or should not be crossed out. This difference of opinion should be expected. The purpose of these exercises is to stimulate discussion about coordination, not to decide who has "right" answers and who has "wrong" answers.

Class Practice

Coordination

1.

HOUSE PETS

   I. Birds
      A. Canary
      B. Vulture
      C. Parrot
      D. Parakeet
  II. Cats
      A. Siamese
      B. Persian
      C. American domestic
      D. Tiger
 III. Domestic
      A. Horse
      B. Skunk
 IV. Dogs
      A. Wolf
      B. Shepherd
      C. Terrier

2.

SPORTS

   I. Team
      A. Football
         1. Touch
         2. College
         3. Tackle
      B. Baseball
      C. Golf
      D. Soccer
  II. Spectator
 III. Individual
      A. Surfing
      B. Hiking
      C. Diving
      D. Jogging
 IV. Two-person
      A. Tennis
      B. Ping-Pong
      C. Badminton

3.

BEVERAGES

I. Nonalcoholic
  A. Milk
    1. Borden's
    2. Whole
    3. Skim
  B. Fruit juice
    1. Orange
    2. Grape
  C. Royal Crown cola
II. Alcoholic
  A. Beer
    1. Schlitz
    2. Budweiser
    3. German
  B. Wine
  C. Scotch and soda
  D. Liquor
    1. Gin
    2. Seagram's 7
    3. Rye

4.

BREAKFAST FOODS

I. Hot
  A. Eggs
    1. Scrambled
    2. Fried
    3. Duck
  B. Meat
    1. Hamburger
    2. Bacon
    3. Sausage
    4. Ham
  C. Oatmeal
II. Cold
  A. Cereal
  B. Fruit juice
    1. Orange
    2. Apple
    3. V-8
  C. Cornflakes
  D. Service
    1. Plates
    2. Cups

Assignment 1

Coordination

1.

THE KITCHEN

  I. Appliances
    A. Large
      1. Refrigerator
      2. Sink
      3. Dishwasher
    B. Manually operated
    C. Small
      1. Mixer
      2. Toaster
      3. Freezer
 II. Table service
    A. Dishes
      1. Plates
      2. Bowls
      3. Spoons
    B. Salt and pepper
    C. Flatware
      1. Knives
      2. Forks
      3. Serving spoons

2.

COLLEGE COURSES

   I. Mathematics
     A. Subtraction
     B. Algebra
     C. Calculus
  II. Social sciences
     A. Psychology
     B. Sociology
     C. Speech
 III. Science
     A. Biology
     B. Botany
     C. Chemistry
 IV. Foreign languages
     A. French
     B. English
     C. German
       1. Grammar
       2. Translation
     D. Spanish

3.

FURNITURE

   I. Living room
    A. Seats
      1. Sofa
      2. Chair
      3. Floor
    B. Tables
      1. Coffee table
      2. End table
      3. Night table
    C. Ashtrays
  II. Bedroom
    A. Bed
    B. Dresser
    C. Chair
    D. Closet
 III. Bathroom
    A. Sink
    B. Toilet
    C. Chair
    D. Bathtub
    E. Clothes hamper

4.

WORD SOUNDS

   I. Begin with *s* sound
    A. Spelled *s*
      1. Salt
      2. Sugar
      3. Sell
    B. Spelled *c*
      1. Copy
      2. City
      3. Cent
  II. Begin with *n* sound,
    spelled *kn*
    A. Knife
    B. Knish
    C. Knit
 III. Begin with *j* sound
    A. Spelled *j*
      1. Jelly
      2. Jingle
    B. Spelled *g*
      1. Gem
      2. Gum
      3. Gin

Assignment 2

Coordination

1.

PUBLICATIONS

I. Periodicals
  A. News magazines
    1. *Time*
    2. *Playboy*
    3. *Newsweek*
  B. Women's magazines
    1. *Cosmopolitan*
    2. *Women's Day*
  C. Newspapers
  D. *Esquire*
II. Books
  A. Literature
    1. Novels
    2. Poems
    3. Catalogs
    4. Dramas
  B. Reference
    1. Dictionaries
    2. Encyclopedias
  C. The Bible

2.

CLOTHING

I. Men's
  A. Suits
    1. Business
    2. Birthday
    3. Leisure
  B. Sportswear
    1. Jeans
    2. Shirts
    3. Jackets
  C. Levi's
II. Women's
  A. Outerwear
  B. Underwear
  C. Pantyhose
III. Infants'
  A. Diapers
  B. Bibs
  C. Blankets
IV. Rock stars'
  A. Silver jeans
  B. Silver boots
  C. Silver lipstick

3.

EXPENDITURES

I. Daily
  A. Transportation
    1. Bus (kids)
    2. Tolls (me)
    3. Car tune-up
  B. Food
    1. Lunch (kids)
    2. Lunch (me)
    3. McDonald's
  C. Coats and shoes
II. Monthly
  A. Newspaper
  B. Electric/gas
  C. Telephone
  D. Vacation
III. Automobile insurance
IV. Bank loan
V. Yearly
  A. Property tax
  B. Income tax
  C. Sales tax

4.

STUDY SUPPLIES

I. Paper
  A. Spiral notebook
  B. Writing paper
  C. Clipboard
II. Writing instruments
  A. Ballpoint pen
  B. Pencil
  C. Eraser
III. Books
  A. Textbooks
  B. Study guides
  C. Library books
  D. Recite and review
IV. Calculator
V. Furnishings
  A. Desk
  B. Lamp
  C. Bed
VI. Special equipment
  A. Typewriter
  B. Slide rule

Lesson 17. Labeling Minor Details

When outlines are written to include minor details, it is possible to combine two or more two-level outlines into one longer outline. *Study* these two-level outlines that contain only major thoughts (Roman numerals) and details (capital letters):

SOCIAL SCIENCE COURSES

I. Sociology
   A. Sociology of the Family
   B. Women in Society
   C. Sociology of Education
II. Psychology
   A. Abnormal Psychology
   B. Human Growth and Development
   C. Psychology of Personality
   D. The Psychology of Aging
III. Anthropology
   A. Cultures and Peoples of Africa
   B. Cultures and Peoples of Asia
   C. North American Indians
   D. Peoples and Cultures of the Caribbean

SCIENCE COURSES

I. Biology
   A. Evolution of Humankind
   B. Anatomy and Physiology
II. Physics
   A. Principles of the Physical Environment
   B. Physics of Life Processes
   C. Basic Atomic and Nuclear Physics
III. Chemistry
   A. Fundamentals of Chemistry
   B. Inorganic and Analytic Chemistry
IV. Geology
   A. Physical Geology
   B. Historical Geology

Now *study* what happens to the numbering and lettering when these two-level outlines are combined to make a three-level outline that has minor details (Arabic numerals):

SOCIAL SCIENCE AND SCIENCE COURSES

I. Social Science
   A. Sociology
      1. Sociology of the Family
      2. Women in Society
      3. Sociology of Education
   B. Psychology
      1. Abnormal Psychology
      2. Human Growth and Development
      3. Psychology of Personality
      4. The Psychology of Aging

Figure 17.1   An Outline That Is Marked to Show How to Check the Logic of an Outline Containing Minor Details

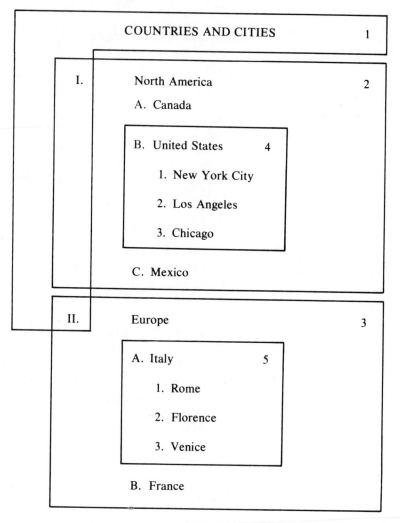

Figure 17.2   A Diagram of an Outline That Is Marked to Show How to Check the Logic of an Outline Containing Minor Details

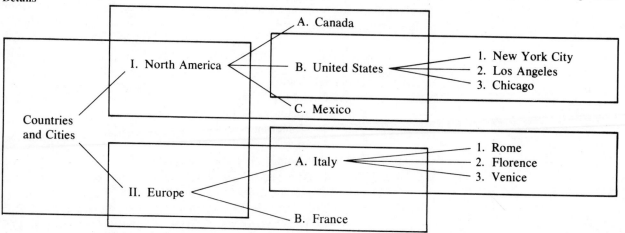

    C. Anthropology
      1. Cultures and Peoples of Africa
      2. Cultures and Peoples of Asia
      3. North American Indians
      4. Peoples and Cultures of the Caribbean
II. Science
    A. Biology
      1. Evolution of Humankind
      2. Anatomy and Physiology
    B. Physics
      1. Principles of the Physical Environment
      2. Physics of Life Processes
      3. Basic Atomic and Nuclear Physics
    C. Chemistry
      1. Fundamentals of Chemistry
      2. Inorganic and Analytic Chemistry
    D. Geology
      1. Physical Geology
      2. Historical Geology

THE LOGIC OF OUTLINES THAT HAVE MINOR DETAILS

When outlines include minor details, their logic is checked in exactly the same way as when they contain major thoughts and details only. The one difference is that minor details (Arabic numerals) are checked against details (capital letters). Interpret the meaning of the boxes over the outline in Figure 17.1 and over the diagram in Figure 17.2.

PRACTICE WITH LABELING MINOR DETAILS

Most students find it easy to label two-level outlines but have more difficulty labeling three-level outlines. Do the problems for this lesson carefully and you will develop a good understanding of how to enter Roman numerals, capital letters, and Arabic numerals into outlines. These are the directions: Do the problems for the minor details of outlines in the same way you did the problems for the major thoughts and details of outlines, *except* label details that logically belong under capital letters with Arabic numerals in the third column of the grid. These are the minor details. Begin with 1 under each capital letter that is followed by minor details. *Also,* you will have the best results in doing the problems for minor details if you

1. enter *all* Roman numerals first,
2. then enter *all* capital letters, and
3. enter *all* Arabic numerals last.

A sample problem has been solved for you to show you how the exercises are done. Be certain that you understand the sample problem before going on to solve the other problems.

    Remember that when the problems in this book are done correctly, they pass the test of coordination (see Lesson 16). Therefore, in doing the problems for this lesson,

1. always use at least two Roman numerals in an outline (I and II);
2. if you use capital letters under a Roman numeral, always use at least two (A and B);
3. if you use Arabic numerals under a capital letter, always use at least two (1 and 2).

Class Practice   *Minor Details*

Some Countries and Cities

I.			Asia
	A.		India
		1.	Calcutta
		2.	Bombay
	B.		China
II.			Africa
	A.		Morocco
		1.	Rabat
		2.	Marrakesh
	B.		Egypt
III.			South America
	A.		Brazil
	B.		Argentina

1.

			North America
			United States
			New York City
			Los Angeles
			Chicago
			Canada
			Mexico
			Europe
			Italy
			Rome
			Florence
			Venice
			France

2.

			Produce
			Fruit
			Apples
			Bananas
			Vegetables
			Potatoes
			Lettuce
			Onions
			Beans
			Dairy
			Eggs
			Cheese
			Swiss
			American
			Milk
			Meat
			Beef
			Hamburger
			Chuck steak
			Pork

3.

			Individual
			Water
			Swimming
			Diving
			Surfing
			Land
			Hiking
			Jogging
			Bicycling
			Two-person
			Table
			Ping-Pong
			Pool/billiards
			Court
			Tennis
			Handball
			Team
			Baseball
			Football

4.

			Prefixes
			Un-
			Unhappy
			Unkind
			Dis-
			Disappear
			Discontinue
			Suffixes
			-ness
			Happiness
			Kindness
			-ance
			Appearance
			Continuance
			Prefixes and suffixes
			Un- and -ness
			Unhappiness
			Unkindness
			Dis- and -ance
			Disappearance
			Discontinuance

5.

			Grooming aids
			Mouth
			Toothpaste
			Mouthwash
			Dental floss
			Hair
			Shampoo
			Conditioner
			Body
			Soap
			Deodorant
			Drugs
			Aspirin
			Laxative
			Iodine
			Beauty aids
			Face
			Lipstick
			Eye shadow
			Hands
			Nail polish
			Hand cream

Assignment 1   **Minor Details**

1.

			Field
			Baseball
			Football
			Soccer
			Table
			Card
			Poker
			Gin
			Rummy
			Boxed
			Scrabble
			Monopoly
			Court
			Racket
			Tennis
			Badminton
			Nonracket
			Volleyball
			Handball

2.

			Nonalcoholic
			Milk
			Whole
			Skim
			Buttermilk
			Fruit juice
			Orange
			Grapefruit
			Prune
			Soda
			Cola
			Root beer
			Alcoholic
			Beer
			Wine
			Californian
			French
			Liquor
			Vodka
			Bourbon

(*continued*)

3.

			Hot
			Cereal
			Oatmeal
			Cream of Wheat
			Eggs
			Fried
			Scrambled
			Meat
			Bacon
			Sausage
			Ham
			Beverages
			Coffee
			Cocoa
			Cold
			Cereal
			Cornflakes
			Puffed Wheat
			Juice
			Orange
			Tomato

4.

			Fall-winter
			November
			Veteran's Day
			Thanksgiving
			December-January
			Christmas
			New Year's Day
			February
			Lincoln's Birthday
			Washington's Birthday
			Spring
			Easter
			Mother's Day
			Memorial Day
			Summer
			Father's Day
			Independence Day
			Labor Day

Assignment 2   *Minor Details*

1.

			Restaurant
			Dining room
			Host
			Waiter
			Busboy
			Kitchen
			Chef
			Baker
			Dishwasher
			Department store
			Sales floor
			Salesperson
			Cashier
			Backrooms
			Wrapper
			Stock people
			Cleaning staff
			Hospital
			Doctors
			Nurses

2.

			Auditory
			Radio
			Phonograph
			Monaural
			Stereophonic
			Quadraphonic
			Lectures
			Visual
			Written
			Books
			Magazines
			Graphic
			Graphs
			Pictures
			Audio-visual
			Television
			Black and white
			Color
			Motion pictures

(*continued*)

3.

			Pie
			Fruit
			Apple
			Cherry
			Peach
			Cream
			Chocolate
			Banana
			Cake
			Fruit
			Angel
			Pound
			Jello
			Fruit
			Ice cream
			Sundae
			Chocolate
			Butterscotch
			Soda
			Shake

4.

			Furniture
			Seats
			Sofa
			Chairs
			Benches
			Tables
			Coffee
			Lamp
			Other
			Bookcase
			Telephone stand
			Accessories
			Walls
			Pictures
			Tapestries
			Table tops
			Lamps
			Ashtrays
			Vases
			Plants

Lesson 18. Common Faults in Labeling Outlines

Three common errors occur frequently when students are learning to use the outline numbering and lettering system.

1. *An A with no B.* The following skeleton outline is incorrect because there is no letter B under Roman numeral I:

> I.
>> A.
>>> 1.
>>> 2.
>
> II.

2. *A 1 with no 2.* The following skeleton outline is incorrect because there is no 2 under the letter B:

> I.
>> A.
>> B.
>>> 1.
>
> II.

3. *Arabic numerals following a Roman numeral.* The following skeleton outline is incorrect because Roman numeral II should be followed by the letter A, not 1:

> I.
>> A.
>> B.
>
> II.
>> 1.
>> 2.

The problems for outlining in this book have been written so you can make outlines with correct subordination and coordination. Therefore, most errors in numbering and lettering can be avoided if you use Roman numerals before capital letters, and capital letters before Arabic numerals. Also, always use at least two Roman numerals (I and II). If you use capital letters, use at least two (A and B), and if you use Arabic numerals, use at least two (1 and 2).

**PRACTICE
WITH RECOGNIZING
FAULTS IN OUTLINES**

The problems for this lesson consist of a skeleton outline under "Start" and three other skeleton outlines to which have been added another symbol—a Roman numeral, a capital letter, or an Arabic numeral. The symbol that has been added is printed in **boldface** type. The problems are solved by examining the symbols printed in boldface type and answering this question:

> Can the symbol printed in boldface type be added in this place to the skeleton outline that appears under "Start" for this problem?

Here follows a sample problem and its solution:

Start:	a. _No_	b. _Yes_	c. _Yes_
I.	I.	I.	I.
II.	II.	II.	II.
III.	III.	III.	III.
A.	A.	A.	A.
	IV.	**B.**	**1.**

a. "No." The IV printed in boldface type *cannot* be added in this place to the skeleton outline that appears under "Start." (An A must be followed by a B or a 1.)
b. "Yes." The B printed in boldface type *can* be added in this place to the skeleton outline that appears under "Start."
c. "Yes." The 1 printed in boldface type *can* be added in this place to the skeleton outline that appears under "Start." (Of course, the 1 will need to be followed by a 2, but you must decide *only* if the 1 can be added in this place—not what needs to follow the 1.)

Solve this sample problem and then read the solution that follows it:

Start:	a. _____	b. _____	c. _____
I.	I.	I.	I.
A.	A.	A.	A.
B.	B.	B.	B.
1.	1.	1.	1.
	II.	**C.**	**2.**

Try to solve the preceding problem before reading the solution. (The answers are: a, no; b, no; and c, yes.) Do the following practice problems in this way.

Class Practice   *Faults in Labeling Outlines*

1. Start: a. _____   b. _____   c. _____

  I.   I.   I.   I.
                  II.   **A.**   **1.**

2. Start: a. _____   b. _____   c. _____

  I.   I.   I.   I.
  II.   II.   II.   II.
      A.   A.   A.   A.
        1.   1.   1.   1.
        2.   2.   2.   2.
      B.   B.   B.   B.
        1.   1.   1.   1.
                  III.   **C.**   **2.**

3. Start: a. _____   b. _____   c. _____

  I.   I.   I.   I.
  II.   II.   II.   II.
                  III.   **A.**   **1.**

4. Start: a. _____   b. _____   c. _____

  I.   I.   I.   I.
  II.   II.   II.   II.
      A.   A.   A.   A.
      B.   B.   B.   B.
                  III.   **C.**   **1.**

5. Start: a. _____   b. _____   c. _____

  I.   I.   I.   I.
      A.   A.   A.   A.
                  II.   **B.**   **1.**

6. Start: a. _____   b. _____   c. _____

  I.   I.   I.   I.
      A.   A.   A.   A.
        1.   1.   1.   1.
        2.   2.   2.   2.
                  II.   **B.**   **3.**

7. Start: a. _____   b. _____   c. _____

I.	I.	I.	I.
II.	II.	II.	II.
A.	A.	A.	A.
B.	B.	B.	B.
1.	1.	1.	1.
2.	2.	2.	2.
	III.	**C.**	**3.**

8. Start: a. _____   b. _____   c. _____

I.	I.	I.	I.
II.	II.	II.	II.
A.	A.	A.	A.
B.	B.	B.	B.
1.	1.	1.	1.
2.	2.	2.	2.
III.	III.	III.	III.
	IV.	**A.**	**1.**

Assignment 1   *Faults in Labeling Outlines*

1. Start: a. _____   b. _____   c. _____

I.	I.	I.	I.
II.	II.	II.	II.
A.	A.	A.	A.
B.	B.	B.	B.
III.	III.	III.	III.
A.	A.	A.	A.
	IV.	**B.**	**1.**

2. Start: a. _____   b. _____   c. _____

I.	I.	I.	I.
II.	II.	II.	II.
A.	A.	A.	A.
1.	1.	1.	1.
2.	2.	2.	2.
	III.	**B.**	**3.**

3. Start: a. _____   b. _____   c. _____

I.	I.	I.	I.
II.	II.	II.	II.
A.	A.	A.	A.
B.	B.	B.	B.
III.	III.	III.	III.
A.	A.	A.	A.
B.	B.	B.	B.
	IV.	**C.**	**1.**

4. Start: a. _____   b. _____   c. _____

I.	I.	I.	I.
II.	II.	II.	II.
III.	III.	III.	III.
A.	A.	A.	A.
B.	B.	B.	B.
1.	1.	1.	1.
2.	2.	2.	2.
	IV.	**C.**	**3.**

(*continued*)

5. Start: a. _____   b. _____   c. _____

I.	I.	I.	I.
II.	II.	II.	II.
III.	III.	III.	III.
A.	A.	A.	A.
B.	B.	B.	B.
C.	C.	C.	C.
D.	D.	D.	D.
1.	1.	1.	1.
2.	2.	2.	2.
3.	3.	3.	3.
IV.	IV.	IV.	IV.
	V.	**A.**	**1.**

Assignment 2   *Faults in Labeling Outlines*

1. Start: a. _____   b. _____   c. _____

I.	I.	I.	I.
A.	A.	A.	A.
1.	1.	1.	1.
2.	2.	2.	2.
3.	3.	3.	3.
4.	4.	4.	4.
B.	B.	B.	B.
C.	C.	C.	C.
D.	D.	D.	D.
II.	II.	II.	II.
III.	III.	III.	III.
A.	A.	A.	A.
	IV.	**B.**	**1.**

2. Start: a. _____   b. _____   c. _____

I.	I.	I.	I.
II.	II.	II.	II.
III.	III.	III.	III.
IV.	IV.	IV.	IV.
V.	V.	V.	V.
A.	A.	A.	A.
1.	1.	1.	1.
2.	2.	2.	2.
	VI.	**B.**	**3.**

3. Start: a. _____   b. _____   c. _____

I.	I.	I.	I.
II.	II.	II.	II.
III.	III.	III.	III.
A.	A.	A.	A.
B.	B.	B.	B.
C.	C.	C.	C.
	IV.	**D.**	**1.**

(*continued*)

4. Start: a. ——————   b. ——————   c. ——————

I.	I.	I.	I.
II.	II.	II.	II.
III.	III.	III.	III.
A.	A.	A.	A.
1.	1.	1.	1.
2.	2.	2.	2.
B.	B.	B.	B.
C.	C.	C.	C.
D.	D.	D.	D.
1.	1.	1.	1.
2.	2.	2.	2.
3.	3.	3.	3.
	IV.	**E.**	**4.**

5. Start: a. ——————   b. ——————   c. ——————

I.	I.	I.	I.
II.	II.	II.	II.
A.	A.	A.	A.
B.	B.	B.	B.
C.	C.	C.	C.
D.	D.	D.	D.
III.	III.	III.	III.
	IV.	**A.**	**1.**

6. Start: a. ——————   b. ——————   c. ——————

I.	I.	I.	I.
II.	II.	II.	II.
III.	III.	III.	III.
A.	A.	A.	A.
B.	B.	B.	B.
1.	1.	1.	1.
2.	2.	2.	2.
C.	C.	C.	C.
1.	1.	1.	1.
	IV.	**D.**	**2.**

Lesson 19. Labeling Outlines

By now you should have a good understanding of the labeling system used in outlines and of the principle of coordination, both of which are essential for making good outlines. The things you do in this lesson will help you understand how the exercises you have done thus far are related to making outlines of written passages.

The exercises require you to place Roman numerals, capital letters, and Arabic numerals in grids, just as you have done in previous exercises. In this lesson, though, the problems are in two parts: (1) a written passage and (2) a grid and listing based on the passage. The types of problems you will do are illustrated by the sample passage and sample grid that follow. *Study* both of them so you can understand how the grid and the written passage are related.

There are two tests an outline will pass if it is a good outline. First, it will be an accurate summary of the information upon which it is based. Second, it will be well organized to show how ideas are related.

When an outline is done in the correct format, it begins with a title. Then, the statements in the outline are correctly numbered and lettered. Major thoughts are labeled with Roman numerals, details are labeled with capital letters, and minor details are labeled with Arabic numerals.

Title: *Outlines*

I.			Pass two tests
	A.		Accurately summarize information
	B.		Organized to show relations among ideas
II.			The correct format
	A.		Begins with a title
	B.		Statements correctly numbered and lettered
		1.	Roman numerals for major thoughts
		2.	Capital letters for details
		3.	Arabic numerals for minor details

The grid is filled in to show there are two major thoughts (I and II). The capital letters and Arabic numerals show how the details and the minor details are related to the major thoughts in the passage.

PRACTICE WITH LABELING OUTLINES

The practice problems for the lesson are done in the same way. When the grids are filled in, they show the relations among ideas in the printed passages.

Class Practice

Labeling Outlines

PASSAGE 1

Students have two basic arguments as to why they should not learn to make notes in the traditional outline format. First, they say it is impossible to make well-organized notes from rambling college lectures. The second claim is that students who underline or highlight well do not need to take notes from textbooks.

However, students who understand the traditional outlining method have an advantage over those who do not. First, if a student can make well-organized outlines, the notes he or she takes from rambling college lectures will be better than the notes of students who have not learned good outline techniques. Second, the assumption that it is always sufficient just to underline in textbooks is not correct; nonetheless, students who understand how to make good outlines will do better underlining in books than those who do not. Finally, college professors frequently ask students to submit outlines for papers they plan to write, and students who understand the traditional outlining method will be able to complete such assignments more easily than students who do not.

Title:

		Arguments against learning to outline
		Can't make good notes from rambling lectures
		Notes not necessary when text is underlined
		Advantages of knowing how to outline
		Can take better notes on rambling lectures
		Can do better underlining in textbooks
		Can make outlines professors request

PASSAGE 2

[Often spelling provides a clue to the pronunciation of the vowel sounds in one-syllable words.]* When there is only one vowel in a one-syllable word, the vowel sound is usually short, as in *hat, bed, win, hot,* and *cut.*

When there are two vowels in a one-syllable word, the vowel sound is often the long sound of the first vowel in the word. Sometimes one of the two vowels is a final silent *e,* as in *hate, kite, hope,* and *cute.* Other times there are two vowels together and the long sound of the first vowel is heard, as the *o* in *boat,* the *e* in *meat,* and the *a* in *pain.*

Title: _____

			One vowel is clue to short sound of the vowel.
			Hat
			Bed
			Win
			Hot
			Cut
			Two vowels provide clue to long sound of first vowel.
			One vowel may be a final silent *e.*
			Hate
			Kite
			Hope
			Cute
			Sometimes there are two vowels together.
			Boat
			Meat
			Pain

* Information in brackets is not outlined.

PASSAGE 3

Each art form puts different demands on artists. Drama requires training of the voice and an ability to recreate life on stage. To excel in ballet, one must have great strength and endurance. A career in opera requires unique natural gifts and a willingness to spend years in training. Unlike these other arts, sculpture requires a talent for composing in three dimensions and a liking for manual labor.

It is interesting how different countries bring a particular art form to mind. Because of Shakespeare, England comes to mind when one thinks of great drama. Russia recalls the performances of its spectacular ballet companies. Italy is synonymous with drama set to the lush melodies of opera and with sculpture of the greatest artists who ever lived.

Title: _____

			Each art form puts different demands on artists.
			Drama
			Training of the voice
			Ability to recreate life on stage
			Ballet
			Strength
			Endurance
			Opera
			Unique natural gifts
			Years of training
			Sculpture
			Talent to compose in three dimensions
			Liking for manual labor
			Countries bring particular art forms to mind.
			England for drama (Shakespeare)
			Russia for ballet
			Italy
			Opera
			Sculpture

Assignment

Labeling Outlines

PROBLEM 1

Among the most frequently misspelled English words are *two, too, to, they're, there,* and *their.* [If you confuse the spellings of these words, you should benefit from the observations made here.]*

The confusion among *two, too,* and *to* may be overcome by remembering three things. First, use *two* only when counting [, as in "*two* heads are better than one"]. Second, use *too* when you intend to say "also" or "overly." For example:

"I hope you will come *too* (also)."
"She is *too* (overly) kind."

Third, use *to* when you cannot use *too* or *two!*

Problems with *they're, there,* and *their* may also be solved rather easily. Use *they're* only when you wish to say "they are" [, as in "*they're* going to the party"]. Use *there* when you wish to say "at or in that place"—for example, "over *there*" or "it's *there*." Then use *their* when you cannot use *they're* or *there*.

If you have difficulty with the spellings of any of these words, you will probably be interested to know that "a lot" is two words, not one word.

Title: _____

			Two, too, and *to*
			Use *two* only when counting.
			Use *too* to say "also" or "overly."
			"I hope you will come *too* (also)."
			"She is *too* (overly) kind."
			Use *to* when you can't use *two* or *too*.
			They're, there, and *their*
			Use *they're* to say "they are."
			Use *there* to say "at or in that place."
			"Over *there*"
			"It's *there*."
			Use *their* when you can't use *they're* or *there*.
			"A lot" is two words, not one.

(*continued*)

* Information in brackets is not outlined.

PROBLEM 2

[There are two important spelling rules that many writers of English never master.]* Many people are not certain when to drop a final silent *e* before adding a suffix to an English root word and when not to drop it. The final *e* is almost always dropped before a suffix that begins with a vowel. For example, the final *e* in *care* is dropped before *-ing* is added to spell *caring*, and the final *e* in *cure* is dropped before *-able* is added to spell *curable*. The final *e* is not dropped before endings that begin with consonants. Thus, the final *e* in *care* is not dropped before *-ful* is added to spell *careful*, and the final *e* in *white* is not dropped before *-ness* is added to spell *whiteness*.

    Confusion also exists about when to change a final *y* to *i* before adding a suffix to an English root word and when not to change it. There are, however, only three simple rules to remember. First, *y* is usually changed to *i* before any suffix if there is a consonant in front of the *y*. Examples are *beauty* and *beautiful, happy* and *happier,* and *silly* and *silliness*. Second, *y* is not changed to *i* when there is a vowel in front of the *y*. Examples are *destroy* and *destroyer, pay* and *payable,* and *annoy* and *annoyance*. Finally, *y* is not changed to *i* before an ending that begins with an *i*. Thus, we have *study* and *studying* and *pretty* and *prettyish* [, not *studiing* and *prettiish*].

* Information in brackets is not outlined.

(*continued*)

Title:

			Dropping and keeping final silent *e*
			Usually drop it if ending starts with a vowel.
			Care plus *-ing* is *caring*.
			Cure plus *-able* is *curable*.
			Usually keep it if ending starts with a consonant.
			Care plus *-ful* is *careful*.
			White plus *-ness* is *whiteness*.
			Changing final *y* to *i*
			When there is a consonant in front of *y*
			Beauty and *beautiful*
			Happy and *happier*
			Silly and *silliness*
			Not when there is a vowel in front of *y*
			Destroy and *destroyer*
			Pay and *payable*
			Annoy and *annoyance*
			Not when adding endings that begin with *i*
			Study and *studying*
			Pretty and *prettyish*

(*continued*)

PROBLEM 3

[You should enter a room to take a test with some concern for how well you will do, yet realizing that excessive concern will prevent you from doing your best.]*

"Test anxiety" will be greatly reduced if you prepare for tests thoroughly, without rushing. Therefore, use the study procedures suggested in this book: mark your textbooks, make notes on what you want to learn, and then thoroughly recite information from texts and lectures. Also, schedule your time wisely so you do not need to cram and so you will arrive at the test room without rushing. The pressure of rushing almost always increases nervousness.

Always try to do your best on tests, but do not place undue importance on grades. First of all, your value as a person is not summed up in a test score. Allow yourself to have areas of weakness and remember that many successful people were not the best college students. Also, you will find that test anxiety lessens and school becomes more rewarding if you do not study for grades alone. Instead, study to increase your knowledge and to develop your thinking skills, thus placing tests in the proper perspective.

Finally, when you take a test, give all your attention to doing the best *you* can do. Do not be concerned with how well others might do on a test; instead, give all your concentration to doing the best *you* can do and evaluate your test performance by comparing it to what you have done in the past—not to what others have done.

* Information in brackets is not outlined.

(*continued*)

Title:

			Prepare thoroughly, without rushing.
			Use good study procedures.
			Mark your textbooks.
			Make notes on what you want to learn.
			Recite thoroughly (texts and lectures).
			Schedule time wisely.
			Don't cram.
			Don't rush into test room.
			Do not place undue importance on grades.
			Your value is not summed up in a test score.
			Allow yourself areas of weakness.
			Many successful people were not great students.
			Don't study for grades alone.
			Study to increase your knowledge.
			Study to develop thinking skills.
			Try to do *your* best.
			Don't be concerned with how others will do.
			Compare your performance to *your* past performance.

Lesson 20. Outlining

The practice problems for this lesson are easier to solve and provide a better learning experience when these things are done:

1. Study Lessons 14 through 19 before you attempt to outline the passages.
2. Follow the directions for outlining that are provided in the next section and your outlines will be more likely to correspond to model outlines. (It will be difficult to understand the directions for outlining if you have not studied Lessons 14 through 19.)
3. Evaluate your outlines using the suggestions in the section of this lesson entitled "Scoring Your Outlines."

DIRECTIONS FOR OUTLINING FOR THIS LESSON

The following directions for outlining have been worked out carefully to help you learn how to make good outlines. If you follow these directions, you will probably be quite satisfied with the progress you make in outlining.

1. *Always use coordination in your outlines.* Lessons 14 through 19 were designed, in part, to help you understand the concept of coordination. When coordination is used:
   a. Outlines have at least two Roman numerals (I and II).
   b. If there are capital letters under a Roman numeral, there should be at least two (A and B).
   c. If there are Arabic numerals under a capital letter, there should be at least two (1 and 2).
   The passages you will outline for this lesson have been selected specifically because good outlines for them are *always* coordinate.
2. *Always subordinate items if they can be subordinated.* You are encouraged to practice subordination at every opportunity; if it is possible to list details next to capital letters or Arabic numerals, you should do so. For example, if both these skeleton outlines could be used for a passage, you should use the one that shows more subordination:

MORE SUBORDINATION	LESS SUBORDINATION
I.	I.
A.	A.
B.	B.
1.	II.
2.	A.
3.	B.
II.	C.
A.	
B.	
C.	

3. *Make your outlines detailed and complete.* When you make outlines for speeches or term papers, you need to give only the major points. However, the primary reason for practicing outlining in this book is to learn to make accurate, complete, and well-organized notes that you can use for study purposes. This is why it is suggested that you make detailed and complete outlines. If you can make detailed and complete outlines, you can also make the summarizing outlines you will need to make for speeches you give and papers you write. Study notes that list only the major points will be of little or no use for study purposes—study notes must summarize accurately the information you want to learn.

4. *Outline information in the order in which it is written in a passage.* Sometimes it is possible to rearrange information into an organization different from the one a writer used. However, this skill is not developed in this book.

5. *Do not outline information enclosed in brackets.* The following sentence is enclosed in brackets: [To help you make good outlines, some information is enclosed in brackets.] Your outlines will correspond more closely to model outlines if you do not outline information enclosed in brackets.

6. *Write titles for your outlines that summarize the information in the passages.*

TYPES OF OUTLINES

In one type of outline all the statements are complete sentences, while in the other type ideas are expressed without using sentences. When you submit outlines for papers you will write or speeches you will give, make an outline using sentences (such as the one on page 107) or an outline that does not use complete sentences (such as the one on page 161). When you make notes for your own study purposes, you may use a combination of sentences and phrases.

SCORING YOUR OUTLINES

While learning to outline, it may be helpful for you to evaluate the outlines you prepare for this lesson. Your instructor can provide you with model outlines so you may score your outlines if you wish. In Figure 20.1 you will find a sample passage and a sample model outline of the type your instructor can provide. An outline may be scored as follows:

1. Score 10 points for a title that summarizes the information in a passage.
2. Score 30 points for Roman numerals if (a) they are in exactly the same number as in the model outline and (b) the information designated by them is the same as the information designated by the Roman numerals in the model outline.
3. Score the points shown for each set of capital letters and Arabic numerals if (a) they are in exactly the same number as in the model outline and (b) the information designated by them is the same as the information designated by the letters or numerals in the model outline.

The points for capital letters and Arabic numerals are distributed so the maximum score for an outline is always 100. If you use this scoring pro-

Figure 20.1   A Sample Passage and a Scored Outline of That Passage

There are two tests an outline will pass if it is a good outline. First, it will be an accurate summary of the information upon which it is based. Second, it will be well organized to show how ideas are related.

When an outline is done in the correct format, it begins with a title. Then, the statements in the outline are correctly numbered and lettered. Major thoughts are labeled with Roman numerals, details are labeled with capital letters, and minor details are labeled with Arabic numerals.

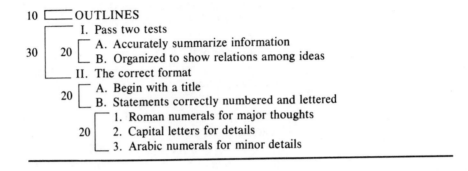

cedure, you will be able to estimate the extent to which your outlines correspond to the model outlines and, thereby, the progress you are making in developing your outlining skills.

PRACTICE WITH MAKING OUTLINES

Use the following ten passages to practice making outlines of the type described in this lesson. Your outlines will correspond closely to model outlines if you follow the suggestions in the section entitled "Directions for Outlining for This Lesson" near the beginning of the lesson.

Problem 1

Outlining a Study Skills Passage

[The word *REAP* is an acronym to help you remember the general rules for taking any test.]

R is for *Read*. Read directions and follow them exactly. Failure to follow directions is a major cause of test grades that are lower than they should be. If a test is in several parts, try to read *all* the directions before answering any questions.

E is for *Easy*. Easy questions are answered first. If you answer easy questions first, (1) you will be certain to answer successfully the questions whose answers you know if you run out of time before you have finished the entire test, and (2) you will build up your test-taking confidence if the test has many difficult questions.

A is for *Answer*. Answer all questions unless you are instructed otherwise. If you answer a question, there is always a chance you will answer it correctly, whereas if you do not answer a question, it will always be marked as incorrect.

P is for *Proofread*. Proofread your answers. Always set aside time for reading your answer sheet or test booklet to make certain there are no carelessly incorrect responses, wrong spellings, or awkwardly constructed sentences in your test.

Problem 2

Outlining a Study Skills Passage

Preparation for a test begins by using all the study skills you know: take good notes, read assigned readings, organize for learning, and review for the test.

You can ask your instructor two important questions that will help you prepare for a test. First, ask what kind of a test will be given. In this way you will know if you should study to write long answers to subjectively scored essay tests or prepare to answer the many detailed questions that might appear on an objectively scored test [such as a true-false or multiple-choice test]. Also, ask what materials will be covered on the test. Some instructors are not helpful in this regard, but others will be happy to clarify exactly which lectures and reading assignments will be used as the basis for test questions.

Be certain to go to class the day a test is given. Frequently, students who fail to take a test on the day it is given never make up the test. Tests that are not taken or made up are usually graded F, for failing.

Finally, take any materials you need to the test room. Instructors cannot fail to be unfavorably impressed by students who arrive for a test without a pen or pencil. In some courses special equipment such as a calculator may be used. There are also times when students are allowed to refer to books during an open-book test.

Problem 3

Outlining a Speech Passage

When you select a topic for a serious speech, it is important to consider the interests of your audience. An audience's interests may be somewhat related to the sex represented. Some topics might not appeal to many women. For example, few women will probably listen with interest to a description of the workings of a car engine or find much fascination in a discussion of how to shop for spark plugs. Among the topics that might not appeal to many men would be the stitching of a buttonhole or the application of facial make-up. Religious and political affiliation are other factors that might determine the special interests of a group you address. Considering these interests of your listeners may help you pick a good topic or avoid a topic that might offend your audience. Finally, consider educational background. A topic that is too specialized, such as a discussion of advanced statistical concepts or the theory of relativity, may be beyond the understanding of almost any audience except one with a highly specialized education. On the other hand, don't pick a topic that is too elementary to be of general interest to your audience.

Problem 4

Outlining a Theater Arts Passage

New York City is the home of theater arts in the United States. The best opera may be seen and heard at the Metropolitan Opera House and the State Theater. In addition, the outstanding ballet companies of the world appear at the City Center Theater and the State Theater. The homes of drama and musical comedy are the city's many Broadway and Off-Broadway theaters.

All of these art forms enjoy great popularity at all times, but each has had peak periods of acceptance. Many opera buffs consider the 1920s as "the golden age of opera" in New York. American drama flourished in the 1950s, when Tennessee Williams and Arthur Miller among others were writing memorable plays, and the 1960s gave us such great musical comedies as "Hello Dolly" and "Fiddler on the Roof." In the 1970s there was more interest in ballet than ever before in the history of the American theater.

You may have been surprised to see musical comedy listed with opera, ballet, and drama as a major theatrical art form. Musical comedy, however, is considered to be the United States' major contribution to the theater arts. The musical comedies of Broadway are produced all over the world, and the songs that have been written for them are popular in many languages.

Problem 5

Outlining an Education Passage

[Some educators believe that objectively scored multiple-choice, true-false, and matching questions are fairer to students than subjectively scored essay tests.]

The critics of essay tests find them to have three important disadvantages. First, they say, the reader of an essay test may be unduly influenced by the writing talent of test-takers. As a result, students with good writing ability may get a high grade on an essay test although they may not have mastered most of the information in a course, and students with poor writing ability may get a low grade on an essay test although they may have a very good understanding of course content. The second major problem, it is argued, is that the "halo effect" has a chance to operate when tests are subjectively scored. For example, an instructor who has the impression that a student is below average might let this impression influence the grading of the student's essay and give the student's good essay a low mark. On the other hand, an instructor who has the impression that a student is very good might give the student's poor essay a higher grade than it deserves. Finally, teachers are known to vary in their opinions, and, consequently, the same answer to an essay question might be graded high by one instructor and low by another.

Those who advocate the use of objective tests say that a primary advantage of such tests is that students are not graded on their writing ability. Also, the halo effect has no chance to operate because an instructor's opinion of a student does not enter into the grading of the student's test in any way. [Either the student's answer is the same as the one given on the answer key, or it isn't.] Finally, since objective tests are scored with an answer key, teachers' judgments of students' scores on a test cannot vary if the answer key is used correctly.

Problem 6   *Outlining an Education Passage*

Test scores are usually used to help determine students' final course grades, but this may be the least important of the four basic reasons for giving tests.

It is good teaching practice to give tests before beginning instruction to determine the extent of students' knowledge or skills in a subject. For example, a writing instructor might ask students to write an essay during one of the first class sessions for the purpose of identifying students who may need special help if they are to do passing work in the writing class. Similarly, an instructor who teaches intermediate algebra may give a test on elementary algebra at the beginning of the term to help determine how many sessions should be devoted to reviewing basic concepts in algebra.

Test scores may also be used to evaluate the amount of progress a student makes in a course. If a student in a writing course wrote a poor essay at the beginning of the term but a very good essay at the end of the term, the student might be said to have made good progress in the writing course. If a student was exhausted after running one lap of a track on the first day of a gymnastics course but ran five laps easily after practicing running in the course, a gym instructor might conclude that the student had made good progress.

Finally, test scores may also be used by instructors to help determine if their instructional methods are effective with students. A test reflects what a teacher believes students should learn in a course. If test scores reflect that students have learned what they were expected to learn, an instructor might judge that his or her methods of teaching are effective. If, on the other hand, test scores reflect that students have *not* learned what they were supposed to learn, an instructor might judge that his or her methods of teaching are not effective. [Of course, these last generalizations do not apply when teachers give tests that are very easy or unnecessarily difficult.]

Problem 7   *Outlining a Business Passage*

[Many businesses have as their primary function the selling of a product or service. Educated consumers understand the steps in the selling process.]

First, the selling businesses want to find buyers. Buyers are attracted to a product or business through advertising, the availability of the product or business, or the efforts of salespeople. Second, the business that is determined to have good sales wants to meet potential buyers under favorable conditions. [There is no point trying to sell something to somebody who is not interested in buying it, and many times people are so interested in buying something that it does not need to be "sold."] Christmas provides a favorable condition for many businesses to sell; vacation periods spur sales for airlines, hotels, and eating establishments. Third, a sales effort is helped when a business presents its product or service to the customer in the most attractive and convincing way possible. Advertising plays an important role in this presentation. Also, manufacturers know that the package in which a product is wrapped or contained can have an important effect on sales.

Once the seller has (1) found a customer, (2) met the customer under favorable conditions, and (3) presented the product to the consumer in an appealing way, the seller must then (4) create the customer's desire to buy. There are two general rules a salesperson follows in attempting to do this. First, if the shopper does not already have the product, the salesperson will try to convince the shopper that life will become richer once the product is owned. Second, if the shopper does already have the product, the salesperson will try to convince the shopper that life will become richer when the old product is replaced with the newer product.

The fifth and final step in the selling process is to close the sale. Once the customer has the desire to buy, the salesperson will do something to get the customer to put out money for the product or service. In retail stores salespeople do this by asking questions such as these: "Will you take the brown shoes or the black ones?" "Is this cash or charge?" "Shall we deliver, or will you take it with you?"

Problem 8   *Outlining a Psychology Passage*

[Neuroses are relatively mild behavior disorders. However, they are sometimes sufficiently disturbing that it is necessary for individuals showing the symptoms of neuroses to seek professional help.]

Anxiety reactions, constituting the most common neurosis, are found in people who have much more tension than average people have. Sometimes people who suffer from this neurosis are overtaken by the strong feeling that something unfortunate is about to happen. This feeling may be accompanied by physical responses, such as weakness, fast breathing, or the desire to vomit.

There are two basic types of obsessive-compulsive reactions: *obsessive thoughts* and *compulsive acts*. Obsessive thoughts are unwelcome thoughts that crowd the neurotic's mind to the extent that they interfere with normal activity. The person may, for example, have recurring thoughts of killing a spouse, jumping out a window, or committing a crime. Compulsive acts often serve the purpose of making a person feel better about obsessive thoughts. A man who has continual thoughts of killing his wife may call her several times a day to check on her well-being; people who have the obsessive thought that they will say something "dirty" may brush their teeth many times a day.

Phobic reactions are uncontrollable fears about dangers that do not exist, or fears that are too great in relation to the danger that actually exists. *Acrophobia* and *claustrophobia* are two of the many phobic reactions. Acrophobia is the excessive fear of height. A person who cannot look out the window of a skyscraper or cannot cross a bridge without extreme discomfort may be suffering from acrophobia. Claustrophobia is the fear of being in small, closed places. A person who cannot enter an elevator or walk into a large closet without experiencing great distress may be a victim of claustrophobia.

Problem 9

Outlining a Psychology Passage

[People with psychoses exhibit severe behavior disorders that almost always require professional help. The two most common psychoses are schizophrenic reactions and manic-depressive reactions.]

Schizophrenia is the most common of the psychoses. *Inappropriateness of emotional response* is one of the symptoms of schizophrenia. This symptom is observed in the schizophrenic who is sad over what would make most people happy, and happy over what would make most people sad. [For example, a schozophrenic man might laugh if told that his home had burned to the ground.] A second symptom of schizophrenia is *withdrawal*. This is observed in schizophrenics who lose all interest in what is going on around them or assume one physical position and do not change this position for hours or days at a time.

Delusions and *hallucinations* are also symptoms that are characteristic of schizophrenic people. Delusions are beliefs in something that is contrary to fact or reality. Schizophrenics may suffer the delusion that their thoughts are controlled by an outside force, such as God or the Devil, or that they themselves are unusually powerful. Hallucinations are the perception (hearing or seeing) of sights or sounds that are not actually present. A schizophrenic may hear voices or see people or objects that are not seen or heard by "normal" people who are with the schizophrenic at the time.

Manic-depressive reactions are found in people who are very happy and excited (manic) at one time and very sad and unhappy (depressed) at other times. In the *manic state* the individual may experience either hypomania or hypermania. *Hypomania* is the mild form of the manic state in which the manic-depressive may never stop talking and may sleep little. *Hypermania* is the intense form in which the individual may scream and be totally out of touch with reality. In the *depressive state* the manic-depressive exhibits these characteristics: little physical activity, discouragement, and tendency toward suicide.

Problem 10

Outlining a Sociology Passage

[There are several ways in which families may be viewed by sociologists.]

A *nuclear family* consists of a married couple and their children. Most people are born into a nuclear family—their family of orientation—and then go on to establish a nuclear family of their own—their family of procreation. The only possible members of a family of orientation are a mother, father, brothers, and sisters. Your family of procreation may include your spouse, sons, and daughters.

The *extended family* is another term sociologists use to describe family relationships. Exactly who is considered a member of an extended family differs from country to country, but in the United States the extended family is usually considered to include children, parents, and other relatives who live with them in the same house or very near by.

Families may also be viewed in terms of the number of partners in a marriage. In our country we have *monogamous families*—there is only one husband and one wife in a marriage partnership. In some societies, though, there are *polygamous families* with more than two marriage partners. Polygyny is the form of polygamy in which there is one husband and two or more wives; polyandry is the form in which one wife has two or more husbands.

[The terms *polygamy* and *bigamy* are often confused. *Polygamy* denotes a marriage pattern that is legal in some societies; *bigamy* is the word used to describe the situation in which a person living in a monogamous society is illegally married to two or more people at the same time.]

Lesson 21. Using Outlining Skills for Studying

In the first lesson for outlining (Lesson 14) it was stated that learning to outline can help you

1. read and understand textbooks,
2. mark textbooks accurately,
3. make notes from textbooks, and
4. make good lecture notes.

Also, of course, learning to outline should help you make better notes on textbooks no matter what note-taking format you use. This lesson provides information and practice so you can transfer what you learned about outlining to reading, marking, and taking notes on textbook passages.

MARKING PASSAGES THAT EXPLAIN TERMS

When textbook passages explain the meanings of terms, it is appropriate to mark them using the underlining or highlighting systems described in Lesson 8. If you *underline,* you should (1) circle terminology, (2) underline definitions, and (3) draw a line alongside examples. If you *highlight,* you should (1) mark terminology in pink, (2) mark definitions in yellow, and (3) draw a yellow line alongside examples.

MARKING PASSAGES FOR IMPORTANT IDEAS

In Figure 21.1 you will find a passage from a psychology textbook that has been underlined to make the important points stand out clearly. Please examine Figure 21.1 to understand how markings can help you organize a textbook for study. If you wish, you may highlight the passage by putting yellow highlighting in the places where lines have been drawn under and alongside words.

Since many different kinds of information might be presented in textbooks, it would be impractical to attempt to describe everything you might want to do to mark a book for study. However, you can use the following suggestions to mark most kinds of information:

1. *Be sparing when underlining or highlighting.* Do not underline or highlight too much information. If you underline or highlight an entire page, it is the same as if you had marked nothing on the page.
2. *Underline or highlight major points.* A major point in a textbook may be stated in a heading or in a sentence. If a major point is in a heading, often it does not need any additional emphasis.
3. *Number important details.* If it is logical to do so, number the details or minor points supporting a major thought so they stand out clearly. Study Figure 21.2 for an example of how circling and numbering may be used

© 1979 by Houghton Mifflin Company

Figure 21.1 An Example of How Important Thoughts May Be Underlined in a Textbook. (From INTRODUCTION TO PSYCHOLOGY Sixth Edition by Ernest R. Hilgard, Richard C. Atkinson and Rita L. Atkinson copyright © 1975 by Harcourt Brace Jovanovich, Inc., and reprinted by permission of the publishers)

Organization and Memory

Memories are patterns of items, woven together by rules that impose varying degrees of *organization;* success in retrieval depends upon how much organization is present. When lists of words or other materials are studied, the greater the degree of organization that the learner can impose on the material, the better the subsequent recall (Mandler, 1974).

Experiment

A dramatic illustration of the effect of organization on memory is provided in the following experiment. The subjects were required to memorize four separate lists of words. For some subjects each of the word lists was presented on a slide in the form of a hierarchical tree, much like the example shown in Figure 8-12. The other subjects studied each of the lists for the same length of time, but the items in each list were arranged randomly on the presentation slide. When tested later, subjects recalled 65 percent of the words presented in a hierarchical organization, but only 19 percent of the same words presented in random arrangements. Further analysis of the data indicated that the subjects who were given the words in an organized form used the hierarchical arrangement as a retrieval scheme for generating recall.

Self-recitation During Practice

Importance

Recall during practice usually takes the form of reciting to oneself. Such self-recitation increases the retention of the material being studied. Suppose a student has two hours to study an assignment that can be read through in 30 minutes. Rereading the assignment four times is likely to be much less effective than reading it once and asking himself questions about the material he has read. He can then reread to clear up points that were unclear as he attempted to recall them. The generalization that it is efficient to spend a good fraction of study time in attempting recall is supported by experiments with laboratory learning as well as by experiments with school learning.

The percentage of study time that should be spent in self-recitation depends on the material and the type of test for which one is preparing. However, the percentage may be higher than our intuitions might suggest. A well-known laboratory experiment indicates that the greatest efficiency in recall of historical material occurs when as much as 80 percent of the study time is devoted to self-recitation. The amount of information recalled increases in proportion to the percentage of study time spent in self-recitation.

Experiment

Advantages

The self-recitation method in ordinary learning forces the learner to define and select what is to be remembered. In addition, recitation represents practice in the retrieval of information in the form likely to be demanded later on. That is, the learner tries to outline a history chapter or provide illustrations of operant conditioning in a fashion similar to what might be expected on an examination. The rule is to begin an active process of recall early in a study period. Time spent in active recall, with the book closed, is time well spent.

Figure 21.2   An Example of Two Ways to Mark the Number of Details Supporting a Major Thought

SOAR

An investigation was undertaken to determine what advice might be given to you to follow when the steps of the SOAR study formula do not help you learn information you want to learn. The conclusions were that (first) you might recite by writing answers on paper rather than by saying them to yourself. It is believed that if writing can help you to learn in mathematics and foreign language courses, it can also help you to learn for other courses. (Second,) you might try constructing a mnemonic acronym or mnemonic sentence. This technique, described in Lesson 5, is widely used by students who have a great deal of information to learn. (Finally,) you can put information into a classification chart when it is logical to do so. When information tells how two or more persons, places, or things are alike or different in two or more ways, it is easier to learn when it is organized in the classification chart format described in Lesson 22.

   However, whether you use the SOAR study formula by itself or together with one or more of these suggestions, it will help you learn whatever you want to learn because it gives you specific things to do to increase your comprehension when you read or listen to lectures, it requires you to decide what you will study, it ensures that you will organize information for efficient learning, and it emphasizes the crucial part of any learning program—*recitation*, which, in simulating test-taking situations, gives you practice at taking tests.

(margin handwriting: What to do when SOAR fails)

(margin handwriting: Advantages of SOAR)

to make the numbers of details stand out clearly in a passage. If you wish, you may highlight Figure 21.2 by putting yellow highlighting in the places where lines have been drawn under or alongside words.

4. *Draw a line alongside examples.* Make examples stand out by drawing lines alongside them, just as you did in Lesson 8.

5. *Write summarizing statements in margins.* Note in Figures 21.1 and 21.2 that lines have been drawn alongside examples, but that sometimes lines have also been drawn alongside information that does not contain examples. When the information alongside a line is not an example, a summarizing statement has been written to point out what kind of information it is. These marginal notes are extremely useful for finding important information while studying. The following words are very helpful to use when writing summarizing statements in the margins of textbooks:

WORDS THAT SUMMARIZE IMPORTANCE

importance of	causes of
advantages of	results of
benefits of	effects of
disadvantages of	evaluation of
problems of	criticism of
reasons for	summary of

WORDS THAT SUMMARIZE DESCRIPTION

types of	contrast between
kinds of	similarities between
characteristics of	comparison between
differences between	parts of

WORDS THAT SUMMARIZE USE, PURPOSE, AND FUNCTION

uses of	steps of
purposes of	methods of
functions of	how to

MAKING NOTES ON TEXTBOOK PASSAGES

It was stated earlier in this book that most successful students use textbook markings to help them make good notes for studying and that they use their notes as the primary source for learning course content. Study the examples of notes in Lesson 9 to review some ways information in textbooks may be well organized for study. Especially examine Figure 9.4 on page 68 to notice that major thoughts stand out clearly and details are listed neatly under them, but that capital letters are not used to label the details. The reason for this is that it is easier to remember there are six things to learn if numerals are used than if letters are used.

PRACTICE WITH MARKING AND MAKING NOTES ON PASSAGES

When you mark textbook passages with underlining or highlighting and when you make notes for them, you should experiment so you may arrive at the methods that are most useful to you when you study. When marking textbooks, you may decide to underline only, to highlight only, or to use a combination of underlining and highlighting along with summarizing marginal notes. When you make notes, you may decide to use study notes only, study cards only, or a combination of study notes and study cards. The practice materials in this lesson are textbook passages you may use for experimentation to decide which marking and note-taking methods are most useful to you.

Consider your markings and notes good when the answers to all these questions are "yes":

1. Do all major points stand out clearly?
2. Are details numbered when it is logical to do so?
3. Are helpful examples clearly marked in books or included in notes?

It is advisable to discuss your solutions with others who mark the passages and make notes for them. Such a discussion will help you understand how the preceding questions can be answered "yes" using a variety of procedures.

The practice problems are arranged in the order of their reading difficulty, with Problem 4 ("Dating") being the most difficult to read. Because of its difficulty, Problem 4 is accompanied by special instructions.

FAMILY RELATIONSHIPS

The relationships between members of a family is a complex subject that interests most people. Since the understanding of family links becomes confusing very quickly, we shall consider only the closest types of relatives: primary, secondary, and tertiary.

Types of Relatives

Primary Relatives. Many people consider an uncle or grandparent to be as close a relative as a brother or sister. The fact is, however, that our *primary relatives* are restricted to the members of our family of orientation (mother, father, brothers, and sisters) and our family of procreation (spouse, sons, and daughters). To understand family relationships, you must learn and remember the seven types of primary relatives.

Secondary Relatives. Your secondary relatives are the primary relatives of your primary relatives, but if people are primary relatives of yours they cannot also be your secondary relatives. For example, your father is a primary relative of your mother—your mother, in other words, is a primary relative of a primary relative. But your mother is not a secondary relative of yours because she is already a primary relative. Your father's brother (your uncle), your mother's father (your grandfather), and your sister's daughter (your niece) are some of your secondary relatives.

Tertiary Relatives. Now that you know the definition of secondary relatives, you should be able to guess the definition for *tertiary* (third-rank) relatives. They are those among the primary relatives of your secondary relatives who, of course, are not already your primary or secondary relatives. Your father's brother's wife (your aunt), your mother's father's father (your great-grandfather), and your sister's daughter's son (your great-nephew) are tertiary relatives.

Blood and Marriage Bonds

Family relationships are complicated by the fact that some people are related to you by blood and others only by marriage. It is for this reason that your mother's brother (your uncle) is a secondary relative, but your mother's brother's wife (your aunt) is a tertiary relative. People related to you by blood are *consanguineous relatives;* those related to you by marriage are *affinal relatives*.

SHOULD YOU USE CREDIT?

WHAT IS CREDIT?

Credit, like cash, is a medium of exchange. It allows you to obtain goods and services or money *now* in exchange for your promise to pay *later*. Credit is the present use of future income.

Credit means using products and services before you pay for them. It is a buy-now-pay-later offer. You are probably using credit right now. Every time you flick on a light switch, take a drink of water, or telephone a friend long distance, you are using credit. This particular form of credit is called *service credit*. We use it every day, but often take it for granted. Do you realize that you are using credit when you pay your newspaper delivery, gas, doctor, or dentist bills? In each case, you use a product or a service before you pay for it.

The term *consumer credit* refers to the use of credit by individuals or families for personal needs. This is different from the credit used for business or agricultural purposes. Consumers in all age groups, income levels, and occupations use consumer credit. If you are a single adult, you probably can pay for most of your personal needs with your income. You may use credit for large expenses such as education, a car, furniture, or a vacation. You might also use charge accounts for convenience in shopping. If you marry, you might use consumer credit to buy furniture, household equipment, or a car, or to pay for educational expenses.

Credit, when carefully used, helps to make life more comfortable and enjoyable. When it is misused, however, credit can cause severe financial problems. You should consider, in adding up the cost of credit, everything you have to give up to use it . . .

HOW CAN YOU GET CREDIT?

When you apply for credit, you are asking the lender to judge your ability to pay the debt. To determine your ability to pay, a salesperson will ask you a lot of questions about you: what your income is, where you live, which bank you use, and what other credit accounts you have. He will probably check your *credit file* also, if you have used credit before. This file tells him what your reputation is for repaying your debts.

A good credit reputation is very important to you as a consumer. Your credit reputation is recorded by a credit bureau, and it is based on three factors:

1. *Capacity* your ability to pay
2. *Character* your willingness to pay
3. *Collateral* your assets

The credit bureau keeps track of your past payment records and your present financial situation to determine your credit reputation. The most important factor is your past record for paying debts. Lenders assume that if you have always paid on time in the past, you are likely to continue making all your payments. Your credit file lasts for seven years. If you file for bankruptcy, it will last for fourteen years. This file is given to any store in which you have a credit account and follows you if you move to another city. Stores, banks, and mortgage lenders can obtain access to your credit file if they are members of the credit bureau, or if they pay a fee in order to use the information for credit purposes. Your credit file is also available to a prospective employer or for present employment purposes including promotion, reassignment, or retention. Your credit file may decide whether or not you obtain a job or receive a promotion as well as obtain credit...

The Fair Credit Reporting Act allows you to see what is in your file and to correct any mistakes you find. It is a good idea to visit your credit bureau and find out what is in your file. If you find a mistake, the credit bureau will check back on their information. If you still don't agree with something in your file, you can give them a short letter (one hundred words or less) to explain the problem. This letter will become part of your credit file.

TYPES AND SOURCES OF CONSUMER CREDIT

There are various sources of consumer credit, including banks, credit unions, insurance companies, finance companies, pawn shops, and stores. The cost of consumer credit differs greatly among these sources. You should compare the various costs just as you do when you buy food or anything else.

Which source is the least expensive? When you buy something at a store, you don't have to get your credit there. You can get a firm cash price for the item, shop around for the best credit, and when you get credit somewhere else, you can pay cash to the store.

When you are comparing costs among the many sources of credit, watch also for different types of credit. It is important to know what your long-term responsibilities are *before* you take them on.

CHARGE ACCOUNT

This can be *either* a thirty-, sixty-, or ninety-day charge account in which you must pay the whole amount in the time given (no interest is charged if you pay in time) *or* a revolving charge account in which you may charge up to a certain amount of money, and you must pay a set minimum amount each month. For example, your limit might be $100, and you may have to pay at least $10 a month. These limits are determined by your income and your credit rating. The interest rate is usually 18 percent per year.

LAY-AWAY

A store might agree to put an item away for you until you have paid for it. You must pay a certain amount at once, and a set amount each week. You can't use the item until you have paid the entire price. There is no charge for this service...

CONDITIONAL SALES CONTRACT

In this contract, although you use the item, the store owns it until it is paid for. If you don't make the payments according to the contract, the store can repossess the item. Depending on state law, the store may either refund the payments you have made or keep them. Usually, the item is sold at an auction. The creditor takes money for the unpaid part of your bill and the expense of repossessing and selling the item. Any money left over is yours. If the auction doesn't raise enough money to cover the creditor's expenses, he may sue you for the remaining money. You could find yourself paying for something you no longer have.

CREDIT CARDS

This is a contract between you and the credit card company. Once you have used a credit card, you have legally accepted the terms—even though you have never signed a contract. Be sure you understand all the conditions of this contract *before* you use the card.

If your card is lost or stolen, you have to pay only up to $50 for charges you did not make. The company can't collect this $50 unless it has told you of this limit and sent you a postage-paid return-addressed envelope for you to use in notifying them of your lost card. Credit cards must have on them some positive identification such as your picture or signature. You are not responsible for cards that have no identification or that you did not specifically ask for.

After making a charge on your credit card, you have a "no-interest" period in which to pay the bill. This period begins on the day the bill was written, not on the day you receive the bill. If you don't pay within this period, you must pay an extra finance charge. If your credit card has an interest rate of 1½ percent per month, you are paying 18 percent interest per year.

CASH OR CREDIT?

Saving your money to pay cash for an item is very similar to using credit and making installment payments. In both cases, the money comes out of your current income and reduces your spendable money. Both methods can be useful ways to improve your financial situation, either by adding to your savings or by reducing your credit debts. Both offer ways to fill a specific need or reach a goal.

There are three main differences to consider when you are deciding whether to use cash or credit. First, using credit costs money, while savings, if they are in a bank, can earn interest money. Second, saving to pay for something in cash means giving up the use of the item until it is paid for. With credit you don't have to wait, but you pay extra for this advantage. The third difference has to do with your personal savings habits. You might find it easier to make monthly payments to someone else than to put money away each month for yourself. If you already have a regular savings plan, then this is not a factor in your decision.

Your decision will depend on your values, needs, income, and alternatives. Consider your personal economic situation and your goals.

Metropolitan Washington

WASHINGTON AS A METROPOLIS

Washington is the capital of one of the world's largest, most influential countries. In population, however, it does not stand out among either the world's capitals or the largest metropolitan areas of the United States. Table 1–1 shows that it ranks fifteenth among world capitals in population. It is smaller than Lima (Peru), Madrid (Spain), and Manila (Philippines), capitals of countries with only a fraction of the U.S. population. Among major metropolitan areas of the world it ranks fortieth, and even in the United States it ranks eighth (Table 1–2). The United States is the most politically and economically powerful country in the world. Why is its capital not the greatest metropolitan center in the world? Let us look at the evidence.

A Special-Purpose Metropolis

Table 1–3 indicates one of Washington's distinctive characteristics as compared with the largest metropolitan areas of the country—those with populations of more than 2 million. The concentration of employment in one activity, government services, is obvious. Notice that government workers in Washington constitute 37.7

TABLE 1-1   METROPOLITAN AREA POPULATIONS OF THE FIFTEEN LARGEST CAPITALS OF THE WORLD

Capital	Population (Millions)	Rank
Tokyo	21.6	1
London	10.7	2
Moscow	10.2	3
Mexico City	9.0	4
Paris	9.0	5
Buenos Aires	8.6	6
Peking	7.6	7
Cairo	6.6	8
Seoul	5.9	9
Djakarta	4.6	10
Delhi	4.5	11
Manila	4.4	12
Madrid	3.6	13
Lima	3.4	14
Washington	3.2	15

SOURCE: Edward Espenshade and Joel Morrison, eds., *Goode's World Atlas,* 14th ed., Rand McNally, Chicago, 1974.

TABLE 1-2   LARGEST METROPOLITAN AREAS OF THE UNITED STATES

(Estimates for Mid-1972)

Metropolitan area	Population	Rank
New York	17,181,000	1
Los Angeles	10,231,000	2
Chicago	7,615,000	3
Philadelphia	5,642,000	4
Detroit	4,684,000	5
San Francisco–Oakland	4,585,000	6
Boston	3,918,000	7
Washington	3,015,000	8
Cleveland	2,921,000	9
Dallas–Fort Worth	2,499,000	10
Houston	2,402,000	11
St. Louis	2,371,000	12
Pittsburgh	2,334,000	13
Miami	2,223,000	14
Baltimore	2,140,000	15

SOURCE: U.S. Bureau of Census, *Current Population Reports,* Washington, D.C., 1976, Series p-25, No. 640.

Reprinted from BETWEEN TWO WORLDS: AN INTRODUCTION TO GEOGRAPHY, 2nd ed., by Robert A. Harper and Theodore H. Schmudde. Copyright © 1978 by Houghton Mifflin Company. Used by permission.

percent of all those employed there. This concentration in a single activity in a metropolitan area is matched only in Detroit, where 37.6 percent of employment is in manufacturing. If we think of Detroit as a specialized manufacturing center, then we must think of Washington as a specialized government center. Its distinctive businesses are the vast array of agencies of the federal government.

The concentration of 30 percent or more of all workers in one activity is not unique to Washington, as you can see from Table 1–3. Six of the other largest metropolitan areas have such concentrations; but in all six manufacturing is the most important activity. Thus Washington not only does not fit the pattern of a major metropolitan area in the United States; it also lacks some of the usual urban nongovernmental functions of other national capitals like London, Tokyo, Moscow, Paris, and even Mexico City and Buenos Aires. They are centers of business, finance, trade, manufacturing, and culture for their countries as well as being capitals. In the United States, however, the major center for such activities is New York City, the largest metropolitan area.

Growth of the Capital

Washington was established specifically to be the seat of national government. Its location was selected primarily because of its proximity to both the geographical center and the center of population of the existing thirteen states from New Hampshire to Georgia. From the beginning, then, Washington's location with regard to other places has been most important. Through the years, Washington has continued to be a key center of transportation routes: first toll roads and sea routes, then a canal system and railroads, and now highways and air routes. Communications have been equally important. It has been necessary to develop systems of transportation and communication that can connect not only with points throughout the United States but also with capitals and large metropolitan centers throughout the world.

TABLE 1-3   EMPLOYMENT STRUCTURE OF MAJOR METROPOLITAN AREAS OF THE UNITED STATES, 1970   (*percent*)

	Total Employment	Manufacturing	Trade	Services	Transportation and Utilities	Construction	Finance, Insurance, Real Estate	Government
New York	4,861,000	20.9	20.9	20.5	7.8	3.5	10.6	15.8
Chicago	2,981,000	31.4	22.5	16.9	6.9	4.0	6.1	12.1
Los Angeles	2,897,000	28.2	22.3	18.9	6.0	3.8	5.9	14.5
Philadelphia	1,796,000	30.5	20.5	17.7	5.8	4.8	5.7	14.8
Detroit	1,483,000	37.6	19.9	14.8	5.3	3.5	4.6	14.3
Boston	1,291,000	21.5	22.7	24.9	5.9	4.0	7.3	13.7
San Francisco–Oakland	1,264,000	16.1	21.3	17.8	10.6	4.8	7.8	21.5
Washington	1,157,000	3.8	19.6	21.8	5.2	5.9	5.9	37.7
St. Louis	899,000	30.5	21.3	16.9	7.5	4.5	5.2	13.9
Pittsburgh	875,000	31.8	20.3	18.3	6.8	4.9	4.3	12.6
Cleveland	859,000	34.5	21.4	16.2	6.0	4.1	4.9	12.8
Baltimore	808,000	24.2	21.9	16.7	7.1	5.4	5.4	19.2

SOURCE: U.S. Bureau of Census, *Statistical Abstract of the United States, 1971*, 92nd ed., Washington, D.C., 1971, Sect. 33.

Washington began as a planned city. Maryland and Virginia ceded an area of ten miles by ten miles to the federal government, which at that time seemed more than adequate for future growth. The original plan covered an area only about three miles by six miles. Even after more than sixty years of growth, the principal means of commuting—horse, carriage, or walking—had not changed, and Washington had yet to reach the limits of the original design. This was the time of the two-story row house that still characterizes much of the District. Houses were tightly placed on narrow lots with no space between them.

By 1917, owing to streetcars and commuter railroads, the city of Washington had spread well beyond the original planned area but not beyond the District boundaries for the most part. Separate suburbs grew in both Maryland and Virginia, where towns had streetcar and commuter railroad connections to Washington. For the first time the District boundaries appeared inadequate for the functioning urban center. The automobile set the pattern for suburbia beyond the District, and today more than two of every three persons in the metropolitan area live in suburban Maryland or Virginia.

A single functioning metropolitan unit has thus sprawled across the original District boundaries. Metropolitan Washington now laps over into the political jurisdiction of two different states, four counties in Virginia and two in Maryland, and five incorporated cities in Virginia and twenty in Maryland.

Population Growth as a
Measure of Governmental Influence

The growth of Washington as the capital city has reflected both the growth of the country and a greater role for the federal government in making the nation function effectively as a unit. In the period of nation building, Washington was a major center of population, ranking eighth among the country's cities in 1850 and ninth in 1880. But its single-purpose character was a limiting factor as business and industry developed throughout the country. By 1920 Washington had fallen to fourteenth place, and not until 1940 did its met-

ropolitan population reach 1 million. Nine cities exceeded it in population at that time.

Since 1940 the metropolitan population of the United States has grown, and Washington has been one of the most rapidly expanding centers. This increase seems directly related to the growing importance of the federal government in the affairs of the country. Federal expenditures in 1940 amounted to only 9 percent of gross national product (GNP); by 1970 they were 30 to 35 percent. Moreover, the higher percentage represented a much larger sum, $313 billion in 1970 as compared with $9 billion in 1940. (The declining value of the dollar accounts for only a small part of this increase.) Although most of this money is actually spent elsewhere, the decisions concerning its allocation and administration are made in Washington. With 2,724,000 employees in 1974, the U.S. government is a huge enterprise, four times as large as General Motors, which is the world's largest private business employer. Between 1940 and 1974 federal employment in Washington more than doubled to 341,000 persons. In this period the total population of the metropolitan area increased two and one-half times.

Problem 4

Marking and Taking Notes on a Textbook Passage

If you use the following questions to guide you as you mark and make notes for Problem 4, you will be more likely to make good markings and notes:

1. According to Gorer, what are the characteristics of dating in this country? Find and number them.
2. According to the passage, what are the major problems of dating? Find and number them.
3. What is the author's major conclusion about each dating problem? Find and mark each conclusion.

THE DATING SYSTEM

…Innumerable accounts have been written about our dating system, but the most interesting—certainly the most provocative—is that penned by Geoffrey Gorer, in his *The American People: A Study in National Character*. Departing from textbook seriousness for a moment, we would like to quote extensively from Gorer. Whether or not you agree with his analysis, you must admit that he had made some telling observations.[18]

According to Gorer, the date begins as an invitation from the boy to the girl for an evening's entertainment, "typically at his expense." The boy "should call for the girl in a car (unless he be particularly young or poor) and should take her back in the car." The entertainment itself depends on the boy's means—anything from an ice cream soda to a lavish meal—but it is usually in a public place and generally involves eating and dancing.

Although "showing the girl a good time" is essential, it is not the primary object of the date. The real object, says Gorer, is for the young man to prove that he is "worthy of love, and therefore a success." And while being a good dancer helps, the necessary signs of approval—predictably—are elicited by talk. "Once again, the importance of words is paramount."

It often happens that on first dates the couple are comparatively unknown to each other. Therefore, Gorer contends, "a certain amount of autobiography is necessary in the hope of establishing some common interest." These life-stories are rather similar to those accompanying any meeting between strangers, except for the "persiflage, flattery, wit, and love-making which was formerly called a 'line' but which each generation dubs with a new name."

Most young men are acutely aware of their "line" and can describe it in great detail. The girl's task, of course, is to parry the "line." "To the extent that she falls for the 'line' she is a loser in

---

[18] Geoffrey Gorer, *The American People, A Study in National Character*, rev. ed., New York, W. W. Norton & Company, Inc. 1964, p. 114.

this intricate game; but if she discourages her partner so much that he does not request a subsequent date she is equally a loser. To remain the winner, she must make the nicest discriminations between yielding and rigidity."

The young man is the winner, says Gorer, if he "is able to get more favors from the girl than his rivals," the proving time being the return trip to the girl's home. "A good-night kiss is almost the minimum repayment for an evening's entertainment," but how much more depends on such things as the expertise of the young man and the attitude of the girl.

The love-making remains emotionally uninvolved, even though the linguistics and behavior are quite similar to genuine love-making. The young man should "prove that he is worthy to be loved by pressing for ever further favors, but the girl who yields too much, or too easily, may well be a disappointment, in exactly the same way as too easy a victory in tennis or chess may be a disappointment. . . . It would be a paradox, but not too great a one, to say that the ideal date is one in which both partners are so popular, so skilled, and so self-assured that the result is a draw."

PROBLEMS OF DATING

In the contemporary (1970–1980) period, dating is an activity in which nearly all young people participate. Participation, furthermore, commences at a rather tender age. In the writer's study of college students, it was found that more than half of both sexes had had their first date before they were 14 years old. In fact, without going into detail, it can be stated that the historical trend in the United States has been toward (1) earlier dating and (2) more dating.

The development of an extensive dating system seems to be a modern-American innovation. In the absence of historical and cross-cultural precedents, therefore, it is only natural to find that the codes have not fully crystallized. Lacking standards of right and wrong, propriety and impropriety, and in the absence of institutionalized patterns of behavior, dating couples have been more or less forced to "make up the rules as they go along." Consequently, dating behavior is often marked by uncertainties and difficulties, not only on the part of the couples involved, but also for parents and other adults charged with the responsibility of regulating conduct norms.

Not all of the difficulties involved in dating stem from the lack of behavioral guideposts. In all ages and in all cultures the socialization of youth has been recognized as a problem involving time and patience. Also, interaction between the sexes—youthful or otherwise—is seldom characterized by total harmony, and

The single's bar—one of the more modern methods of meeting partners and socializing. (Rick Smolan, Stock Boston)

it is hardly to be expected that dating relations would be an exception. All things considered, when these "natural" difficulties are augmented by a scarcity of behavioral rules, it is little wonder that problems arise. While it is by no means exhaustive, the following summary is probably representative of the kinds of issues that have come to be associated with the American dating system.

Parental Influence.　There can be no doubt that parents exert a fairly strong influence on the dating and courtship activities of their children. Numerous studies in the last 30 years all confirm the fact. There is also no doubt that this influence leads to a measure of conflict between young people and their parents, particularly in the case of teen-agers. In the present writer's study of 1,079 college students, the question "Have you ever had arguments or conflicts with either of your parents regarding persons you have dated?" revealed that over 50 percent of the females and nearly 40 percent of the males answered in the affirmative.

Whether parents should or should not express their feelings on the subject is an open question, although certainly one could argue that failure to voice an honestly held opinion may be just as harmful as voicing one. In practice, most parents do feel impelled to speak out, and many young people feel just as impelled to resent the "intrusion." As a matter of fact, modern movies—which routinely seem to side with the young people—are likely to depict parental advice as "interference."

In everyday life, however, do parents really exercise poor judgment concerning their sons' and daughters' choice of a mate? Or is their advice likely to be sound? Findings based on empirical investigation indicate that the judgment of parents is beneficial rather than harmful, although in recent years there has been a paucity of research aimed at answering the question. But, irrespective of the evidence, it is likely that conflict between parents and children over dating and marital selection will remain. Such conflict must be written off as one of the prices of a relatively free dating system.

Interreligious and Interclass Dating.   Closely related to the problem of parental influence is the question of dating persons of a different faith or of a different socio-economic level. If young people were entirely free in the matter of dating and marital selection, it is likely that problems relating to religion and social class would be minimal. But the fact of the matter is that parents and relatives do exert influence, and in most cases they take a dim view of so-called exogamous marriages.

Parents who caution their children against dating someone from a lower social stratum are not necessarily being snobbish, and mothers and fathers who remonstrate with their children on the dangers implicit in interreligious dating are not necessarily bigoted. In both instances, parents may be motivated by a sincere belief that exogamous marriages are not successful. They may feel that, once two people have fallen in love it is usually too late to do much about it, and hence the logical thing is to refrain from interdating in the first place.

Young people are usually more liberal than their parents insofar as the above-mentioned factors are concerned, so that it is almost inevitable that interreligious and interclass dating should lead to a certain amount of conflict within the home. Over the years, it would be expected that such conflict might diminish, since theoretically the liberal attitudes of youth should persist as they grow older. What seems to happen, though, is that the views of young people become less and less liberal as they grow older, and by the time they themselves are parents it is likely that they, too, will take a dim view of exogamous marriages.

The Lack of Physical Attractiveness.   Throughout the world, physical appearance is of some importance, even though it may not be considered so crucial as intelligence or personality. In a society that exalts romantic love, however, physical attractiveness is of special significance, particularly in the case of young people, whose very marriageability often depends on "looks." With the faces of glamorous stars beaming from movie and television screens, with newspaper ads, magazine covers, and billboards flooded by pictures of handsome men and beautiful women, a social historian might well characterize the present era as the age of The Face. And whatever the impact on society at large, it can hardly be doubted that young people are susceptible to the veritable onslaught of physical charm. Whether adults like it or not, the daydreams of youngsters are quite likely to involve physical attributes of handsomeness and beauty.

Since men are more readily influenced by physical attractiveness than are women, "good looks" have become a fetish with many an American girl. And, in view of the value our culture places on beauty, this particular feminine emphasis may not be entirely misplaced. Figuratively, and in some ways almost literally, the pretty girl in our society is accorded the role of queen.

But what society giveth with one hand it taketh away with the other, for, if the pretty girl is placed on a pedestal, the unattractive girl is likely to find herself shunned. By adult standards, young people are often cruel in their social treatment of others, and nowhere is this fact more apparent than in the dating situation. With our cultural emphasis on The Face, young people—boys especially—have a tendency to overlook the underlying facets of personality and character, even though in a formal sense they may have been taught otherwise. Lack of physical attractiveness, therefore, is one of the most serious of our dating problems; indeed, from the point of view both of the number of individuals affected and the extent to which they are affected, it may well be the most serious.

While girls may be penalized more than boys, neither sex can escape the humiliation that too often accompanies homeliness, facial deformity, bad complexion, defective teeth, and the like. Individuals so afflicted sometimes retreat from the dating front altogether, rather than suffer continued—and in their own view unjust—rejections. Young people have a need for emotional security (more so, perhaps, than at any other time in life), and it is unfortunate that our dating system sometimes hinders rather than helps the situation.

Like most of the other difficulties associated with dating, there is no ready solution to the problem. One possible, if unlikely, solution would lie in a change of emphasis in our mass media, whereby The Face would be considered less important than The Person. More societal emphasis in this direction, certainly, would help to alleviate a chronic problem associated with dating.

(Burk Uzzle, Magnum Photo)

Social Awkwardness. It is a common observation that most youth, especially those in their early teens, are somewhat awkward and ill at ease in their associations with the opposite sex. The boys may be loud and gesticulatory, and the girls may giggle and laugh continually, but these are often signs of tenseness rather than composure, however much the participants try to give the appearance of poise. In fact, research findings indicate that young people of both sexes are keenly aware of the problem.

All things considered, it is perhaps a wonder that teen-agers do as well as they do. Many adults are by no means at ease on social occasions, and at some time or another practically *all* adults have difficulty thinking of an appropriate remark to make. At any rate, it is easy to understand why young people have conversational difficulties, and why solitary dating couples so often run out of things to talk about. Conversational adeptness hinges in part on the scope of personal experience, and one of the reasons adults are better conversationalists than young people is that the former have a fund of knowledge and a storehouse of personal experiences to draw from. Also, the art of conversation, like other social graces, takes practice. And if, in this respect, dating situations are sometimes painful, they are seldom traumatic. While it may seem disheartening at the time, social awkwardness can hardly be considered a major problem.

Sexual Involvements.   Although many adults have succeeded in closing their eyes to the fact, sex has become an important part of the general dating pattern. While the goal of dating may not be primarily sexual, it is probably safe to say that there are relatively few dates wherein the sex problem does not make itself felt in one way or another.

If the couple indulge in some sort of sexual activity, there may be feelings of remorse and guilt. If they abstain altogether, there may be feelings of frustration. If they have intercourse, there is always the possibility of pregnancy. Verily, it would seem that all roads lead to some sort of conflict.

The whole question of sex during dating represents something of a paradox. On the one hand, it has become almost customary to shut our eyes to the issue and to pretend that no problem exists; at least, the subject is rarely mentioned in polite company. On the other hand, as judged by the number of words written about it in books and magazines—to say nothing of the number of plays and films on the subject—the premarital sex problem is of extreme importance. It will probably be many, many decades before societal views on the subject have become crystallized to the point where a consensus can be said to exist. In the meantime, the premarital sex issue will continue to plague a fair percentage of dating couples.

Lesson 22. Classification Charts

**THE FORM OF
CLASSIFICATION CHARTS**

Most note-taking methods are fundamentally the same—major thoughts are made to stand out and minor thoughts are listed under them in some way to show that they are subordinate. This is true of lecture notes (Lesson 4), study notes and study cards (Lesson 9), and outlines (Lesson 20). Classification charts, however, are fundamentally different in appearance. Figure 22.1 shows a classification chart that was made for the following passage:

THE PSYCHOSEXUAL STAGES, ACCORDING TO FREUD

Sigmund Freud proposed that there are five stages in people's psychosexual development. He believed that the success with which individuals deal with the problems of each stage is related to their personality development.

The first stage, which lasts from birth until about one year of age, he called the *oral stage*. During this time the infant's pleasure centers around the mouth in eating, biting, chewing, and sucking. The *anal stage,* which lasts from age one year to age three, is the time when the young child finds pleasure in holding and letting go of waste matter from the body. This is the important time of toilet training. The *phallic stage* begins at age three and continues until age six. It is during this time that the child, male or female, derives pleasure from primary sex organs to a great degree. Beginning at age six and continuing until about age eleven, the child passes through what Freud called the *latency period*. During this time the child denies affection and attraction for the parent of the opposite sex and identifies strongly with the parent of the same sex. Adolescence marks the beginning of the *genital stage,* which is the awakening of sexuality and the desire for heterosexual love.

You are familiar with classification charts because you have seen them in your textbooks for years. Textbook writers use classification charts to clarify confusing information and make it easier to understand. You can make classification charts of your own to learn certain kinds of information that would be more difficult to learn in other forms. It is easier to learn the information about Freud's psychosexual stages from the classification chart than from an outline. Note how much better the stages, ages, and characteristics of psychosexual development stand out in the classification chart in Figure 22.1 than in the following outline:

Figure 22.1 An Example of a Classification Chart

The Psychosexual Stages, According to Freud

	Age	Characteristics
Oral Stage	Birth to 1 year	Gets pleasure from mouth by sucking, eating, biting, and chewing.
Anal Stage	1 year to 3 years	Gets pleasure from holding and letting go of body waste.
Phallic Stage	3 years to 6 years	The child derives pleasure from his or her own primary sex organs.
Latency Period	6 years to about 11 years	Child denies attraction for parent of opposite sex and identifies with parent of the same sex.
Genital Stage	Adolescence	Awakening of sexuality and desire for heterosexual love.

THE PSYCHOSEXUAL STAGES, ACCORDING TO FREUD

I. Oral stage
  A. Birth to one year
  B. Gets pleasure from mouth by sucking, eating, chewing, and biting
II. Anal stage
  A. One to three years
  B. Gets pleasure from holding and letting go of body waste
III. Phallic stage
  A. Three to six years
  B. Child derives pleasure from his or her own primary sex organs.
IV. Latency period
  A. Six years to about eleven years
  B. Child denies attraction for parent of opposite sex and identifies with parent of same sex.
V. Genital stage
  A. Adolescence
  B. Awakening of sexuality and desire for heterosexual love

Whether or not information can be put into a classification chart is determined by answering this question: *Does this information explain how two or more persons, places, or things are the same or different in two or more ways?* If the answer is "yes," the information may be placed in a classification chart for studying. The information about Freud's psychosexual stages could be put into a classification chart because it explains how five stages of development (more than two things) are different with regard to age and characteristics (two ways).

THE USES OF CLASSIFICATION CHARTS

In some courses classification charts are indispensable learning aids. Biology is the classic example because one of its primary purposes is to explain the similarities and differences among various plants and animals. However, classification charts can be important study tools in any course. In all subject areas persons, places, or things are shown to be alike or different in two or more ways. Following are two examples of how classification charts might be made in order to learn information.

A Classification Chart for History. In history you might make a classification chart to study several battles with regard to when they were fought, where they were fought, who fought them, and their outcomes. A chart for such information might be set up in the way shown in Figure 22.2.

A Classification Chart for Music. In a music course you might make a classification chart to learn how some musical pieces are alike or different with regard to their composers, dates of composition, the musical styles they represent, and their impacts on the history of music. Figure 22.3 shows an example of how a chart might be made to learn such information.

Figure 22.2 An Example of a Classification Chart That Might Be Made for a History Course

Civil War Battles

	Sumter	Bull Run	Fredericksburg	Gettysburg
Date				
Southern Troops				
Northern Troops				
Outcome				

Figure 22.3 An Example of a Classification Chart That Might Be Made for a Music Course

Operas

	Composer	Date	Style	Importance
Dafne				
Orfeo				
Zauberflöte				
Fidelio				
Tristan				
Carmen				

The possibilities for classification charts are endless because almost all writers make comparisons of one sort or another, whether they are directly stated or implied.

PRACTICE WITH MAKING CLASSIFICATION CHARTS

Do the following practice problems using these directions:

1. Read a passage.
2. Ask yourself, "What items are being compared?" Use the answer to this question to write the labels for the rows of the chart. (The rows are labeled down the lefthand side.)
3. Then ask yourself, "On what bases are these items being compared?" Use your answer to this question to write the labels for the columns of the chart. (The columns are labeled across the top.)
4. Fill in the boxes of the chart with the appropriate information.
5. Write a title for each chart.

Problem 1   ***Classification Charts***

SHELDON'S SOMATOTYPES

One of the most interesting systems created to classify people is the one devised by William H. Sheldon, which has as its purpose to predict people's personality characteristics by identifying their body types. Sheldon's somatotypes (body types) are composed of three basic components. The *endomorph* component is the fatness and roundness found in many people; the *mesomorph* component is strong muscle and rectangular bone structure; and the *ectomorph* component is characterized by thinness and flatness of body. Though no one person is usually a pure endomorph, mesomorph, or ectomorph, each component is said by Sheldon to carry distinctive personality traits. To the extent that people are endomorphic, they enjoy the company of others and seek comfort; to the extent that people are mesomorphic, they are aggressive and fearless; and to the extent that people are ectomorphic, they are socially inhibited and unlikely to enjoy physical competition.

Problem 2

Classification Charts

THE GREEK TEMPERAMENTS

One of the oldest of type classifications, that of temperament, goes back to the ancient Greeks. The four types—*sanguine, phlegmatic, melancholic, and choleric*—were based on the prominence of one of four "body fluids": The sanguine person, generally warm hearted and pleasant, had a prominence of blood; the qualities of the phlegmatic person, listless and slow, were attributed to phlegm; the melancholic person, suffering from depression and sadness, had too much black bile; the choleric person, easily angered and quick to react, was influenced by his yellow bile.*

* From INTRODUCTION TO PSYCHOLOGY Fifth Edition by Ernest R. Hilgard, Richard C. Atkinson, and Rita L. Atkinson copyright © 1971 by Harcourt Brace Jovanovich, Inc., and reprinted by permission of the publishers.

Problem 3   *Classification Charts*

SOCIAL CLASS

The pioneering work in social class was done by W. Lloyd Warner and his colleagues in their studies of American communities. Richard Coleman, one of Warner's associates, characterized the six social classes:

1. *Upper-Upper.* This is the smallest of the classes, with less than 1 percent of the population of a community. It is comprised of families who have been prominent in the town or city for two or three generations and who are concerned with "living graciously, upholding the family reputation, reflecting the excellence of one's breeding, and displaying a sense of community responsibility."

2. *Lower-Upper.* Approximately 2 percent of a community is comprised of people who have acquired wealth recently. They are likely to be founders of large businesses, executives of important companies, and newly rich doctors and lawyers. Their goals are to live graciously and pursue success.

3. *Upper-Middle.* The 10 percent of a community in this class is likely to be college educated. They tend to be "moderately-successful professional men and women, owners of medium-sized businesses, and 'organization men' at the managerial level." They are concerned with having successful careers and reflecting this success in their homes and social relationships. The major difference between the Upper-Middle and Lower-Upper class is the degree of success they have achieved and the extent to which they reflect this in their lifestyles.

4. *Lower-Middle.* Somewhere between 30 and 35 percent of a community may be described as being "at the top of the 'Average Man's World'." They are likely to be white-collar workers, small businessmen, and high-status blue-collar workers. Respectability and striving characterize the members of this class. They live in comfortable homes in the "right" part of town, shop in "good" stores, plan for the college education of their children, and are active in clubs and churches.

5. *Upper-Lower.* With nearly 40 percent of a community, this is the largest of the six classes. These are the semiskilled workers on assembly lines and at thousands of other essential jobs. Though they may make good money, they are more interested in "getting by" and in "enjoying life" than they are with respectability and planning for the future.

6. *Lower-Lower.* The remaining 15 percent of a community is comprised of the unskilled and underemployed. Opportunity is limited for these people. Their outlook on life is that they cannot change their condition and there is no reason for attempting to do so.*

---

* Reprinted, with adaptations, from Richard Coleman, "The Significance of Social Stratification in Selling," in *Marketing: A Mature Discipline,* edited by Martin Bell, 1961, published by the American Marketing Association.

Problem 4

Classification Charts

Read the following passage and show how Eysenck's two-dimensional scale and the Greek temperaments (Problem 2) are related.

1. Label the columns of the chart with two of Eysenck's dimensions.
2. Label the rows of the chart with the other two dimensions.
3. Fill in the boxes with the words *phlegmatic, choleric, sanguine,* and *melancholic* to show how Eysenck's classification system is related to the Greek temperaments.

EYSENCK'S TWO-DIMENSIONAL THEORY

Eysenck has proposed that many important aspects of personality can be understood through a combination of two dimensions: stable-unstable (sometimes called normal-neurotic) and introverted-extraverted. If one divides these dimensions at the midpoint of the distributions (half the subjects being higher or lower on each of the dimensions), four personality types emerge:

Stable-Extravert   Unstable-Extravert

Stable-Introvert   Unstable-Introvert

Before proceeding to characterize these types, something may be said about the component dimensions.

The terms "extraversion" and "introversion," while not originated by him, owe their popularity to Carl J. Jung (1875–1961), a prominent Swiss psychologist who was originally a follower of Freud, but later developed his own system of analytic psychology. The introvert tends to withdraw into himself, especially in times of emotional stress or conflict. Characteristics of introversion include shyness and a preference for working alone. The introvert may take to the speaking platform, as in the leading of a religious movement, but even then he is impelled from within. The extravert, by contrast, when under stress tends to lose himself among people. He is likely to be very sociable, a "hail fellow well met." He tends to choose occupations such as sales or promotional work, in which he deals with people rather than with things. He is likely to be conventional, well-dressed, outgoing. It is not difficult to find among our acquaintances a "typical" introvert or a "typical" extravert. This gives such a classification plausibility and accounts for its popular appeal (Jung, 1923).

The other dimension, stability-instability, simply means that at the stable end are people whose emotions are controlled and not easily aroused, who are generally calm, even-tempered, and reliable; at the other end are those who are "moody, touchy, anxious, restless" (Eysenck and Rachman, 1965).*

* From INTRODUCTION TO PSYCHOLOGY Fifth Edition by Ernest R. Hilgard, Richard C. Atkinson, and Rita L. Atkinson copyright © 1971 by Harcourt Brace Jovanovich, Inc., and reprinted by permission of the publishers.

Part 4. Test-Taking Skills

This part of the book gives basic information and opportunities for practice that should help you become more skillful at taking college tests.

Tests are often thought of as being of two basic types: *objective* or *subjective*. One way to distinguish between objective and subjective tests is to think of objective tests as those for which answer keys may be prepared and subjective tests as those for which no answer keys may be prepared.

Multiple-choice, true-false, spelling, and mathematics tests are examples of objective tests. A question on such tests has only one answer that is considered correct. The correct answer may be put in an answer key, and anyone who uses the answer key correctly to score students' answer sheets will give students the same test scores.

Essay tests are tests for which students write long, written answers, and they provide the classic example of the subjective test. It is extremely difficult, or impossible, to make answer keys for essay tests because students' answers are likely to be quite varied. Therefore, such tests are graded on the basis of instructors' subjective reactions to students' answers. Instructors are likely to disagree on the grades that should be given to students for their answers on essay tests. It is for this reason that essay tests are often called subjective tests.

The lessons in Part 4 are grouped under the main headings "Objective Tests" and "Essay Tests," as shown at the left.

Lesson 23. An Approach to Objective Tests

For the most part, *objective tests* are either multiple-choice tests, for which students write "a," "b," "c," or "d" for answers, or true-false tests, for which students write "T" or "F" for answers; and essay tests are tests for which students give long, written answers. Since the skills needed for taking objective tests are somewhat different than the skills needed for taking essay tests, objective tests are discussed in this lesson and essay tests are discussed in Lesson 28. Practice to help you become better at taking objective tests is given in Lessons 24 through 27, and practice for essay tests is given in Lesson 29 and 30.

**HOW TO TAKE
OBJECTIVE TESTS**

Many times when instructors return answer sheets for objective tests and discuss the answers in class, students see several incorrect answers that they know they should have answered correctly. They sometimes feel they should have received a grade higher than the one they earned. If you have ever had this feeling, you will experience it less often when you use the suggestions in this lesson for taking objective tests.

Be Certain You Understand the Test Directions. When you take a multiple-choice test, you have good reason to believe that you should select the best choice for the answers to the items. Likewise, when you answer true-false questions, you assume that you are to mark true statements as "true" and false statements as "false." However, you should not always go on these assumptions; there are many variations in what you may be asked to do in responding to multiple-choice or true-false questions.

For example, some college professors require that when true-false statements are marked "false," students must make a written statement about why they are false. Students who do not follow this direction lose points on their test scores. This variation is only one of many for objective tests. The important thing to remember is that you should *read test directions carefully,* and if anything is unclear to you, you should ask your instructor for clarification before proceeding with the test.

Answer Questions on the Basis of What You Know or Understand. Sometimes when students are taking multiple-choice tests, they decide that the correct answer to an item is *d,* but do not write "d" on their answer sheet because they feel they have already written too many *d*'s. Other times they decide that the correct answer is *a,* but do not write "a" because they suspect the instructor is trying to "trick" them. These students are using poor test-taking skills.

The purpose of college tests is to find out what students know about course content. Thus, you should always try to answer questions on the basis of what you know and try to show that you understand the things you were supposed to learn. Most college professors do not deliberately write questions to trick students. They try to write questions that will be answered correctly by students who have learned the information in a course and incorrectly by those who have not.

When in Doubt About a Correct Answer, Give the Answer You Believe Is Intended by the Person Who Wrote the Question. Sometimes, even though you are thoroughly prepared for a test, you will encounter test items that are difficult to answer. When this happens, you should consider carefully which answer is most likely to be marked correct by the person who wrote the question. For example, in a sociology course some students had difficulty choosing between answers *a* and *c* for this test item:

> Marijuana use
> a. is strongly associated with hard drug use.
> b. is never associated with heroin or LSD use.
> c. is not strongly associated with hard drug use.
> d. has no social or political ramification.

The reason for their difficulty was that the textbook had two accounts: one from a group of researchers who had found a strong association between marijuana use and hard drug use and another from a group of researchers who had not found a strong association between uses of the two. And the students failed to take into consideration what their instructor had said about this research during a class lecture. The instructor had made it very clear in class that the research that found *no* strong link between marijuana use and hard drug use was more convincing than the other research. The students who considered what their professor had said selected *c* as the answer to the question, and their choice was marked correct.

Your college professors are going to ask you many questions that you will answer correctly only if you consider carefully what they intend the correct answers to be. When you are in doubt about the correct answer to a test item, try to figure out what is intended as the correct answer by the person who wrote the item.

Answer the Easy Questions First. If you were to observe a group of first-year students taking an objective test, you would notice that most of them approach the test by answering test questions in the exact order in which they are presented. But if you were to watch a group of juniors taking the same test, you would see most of them answering the easy questions first and saving the difficult ones for later consideration. Through test-taking experience the juniors have learned three valuable facts:

1. If they answer the easy questions first, they will be certain to answer all the questions they know if time runs out before they are able to complete the test.

2. They may find the answer to a question they do not know when they read the other questions on the test.
3. They will build up their test-taking confidence by answering questions they know at the beginning of the test-taking session.

You may be able to benefit from what these experienced test-takers have learned. When you take a multiple-choice test, for example, go through the test reading each item carefully, but answering only the questions for which you are certain you know the correct answers. If there are forty questions on a test, you may answer only twenty of them the first time you read through the test. Then go back and reread each unanswered question, answering as many as you can the second time through the test. Repeat this procedure until you have answered all the questions.

Answer All the Questions on an Objective Test Unless There Is a Penalty for Guessing. The scores for most college tests are found by adding up the number of correct answers to questions. Even when you are not certain of a correct answer to a question, you should guess at the answer because there is always a chance that your guess will be correct.

In Figure 23.1 you will find an answer sheet for a true-false test. Of the 50 questions, 34 have been answered correctly, but the student who is taking the test must make wild guesses at the answers to the remaining 16

Figure 23.1 Answer Sheet for a True-False Test. The student has a score of 68 because 34 of the 50 questions are answered correctly (2 × 34 = 68). Make wild guesses at the answers to the other 16 questions. Add the number you guess correctly to 34 and multiply by 2 to find the new score. The answer key is on page 207.

1. T	11. F	21. ___	31. F	41. ___
2. T	12. F	22. F	32. F	42. T
3. ___	13. ___	23. T	33. F	43. F
4. F	14. F	24. ___	34. ___	44. ___
5. T	15. ___	25. ___	35. T	45. ___
6. ___	16. F	26. T	36. T	46. T
7. T	17. F	27. T	37. F	47. F
8. T	18. ___	28. ___	38. F	48. F
9. ___	19. T	29. ___	39. T	49. T
10. F	20. F	30. T	40. ___	50. T

Figure 23.2   Answer Sheet for a Multiple-Choice Test. The student has a score of 68 because 34 of the 50 questions are answered correctly (2 × 34 = 68). Make wild guesses at the answers to the other 16 questions. Add the number you guess correctly to 34 and multiply by 2 to find the new score. The answer key is on page 207.

1. _a_	11. _d_	21. ___	31. _b_	41. ___
2. _c_	12. _c_	22. _c_	32. _d_	42. _a_
3. ___	13. ___	23. _d_	33. _d_	43. _a_
4. _c_	14. _d_	24. ___	34. ___	44. ___
5. _b_	15. ___	25. ___	35. _c_	45. ___
6. ___	16. _a_	26. _d_	36. _a_	46. _c_
7. _d_	17. _c_	27. _a_	37. _b_	47. _a_
8. _d_	18. ___	28. ___	38. _b_	48. _b_
9. ___	19. _a_	29. ___	39. _c_	49. _a_
10. _b_	20. _b_	30. _d_	40. ___	50. _b_

questions. There are only two possible answers for true-false questions, so the student guessing at the answer to a question has a 50-percent chance of guessing the correct answer. Since 34 questions are already correctly answered, the student has a score of 68 (D+). But, by chance, the student may guess 8 answers correctly and add 16 points to the test score, bringing it up to 84 (B). Of course, by chance, the student may guess either less than 8 or more than 8 answers correctly. Make wild guesses for the answers to the 16 unanswered true-false questions in Figure 23.1 to see how many you guess correctly.

In Figure 23.2 there is an answer sheet for a multiple-choice test. Of the 50 questions, 34 have been answered correctly, but the student who is taking the test must make wild guesses at the answers to the remaining 16 questions. There are four possible answers for the multiple-choice questions (a, b, c, or d), so the student guessing at the answer to a question has a 25-percent chance of guessing the correct answer. Since 34 questions are already correctly answered, the student has a score of 68 (D+). But, by chance, the student may guess 4 answers correctly and add 8 points to the test score, bringing it up to 76 (C). Of course, by chance, the student may guess either less than 4 or more than 4 correct answers. Make wild guesses for the answers to the 16 unanswered multiple-choice questions in Figure 23.2 and see how many you guess correctly.

The following are the correct answers to the unanswered questions in the true-false test (Figure 23.1) and the multiple-choice test (Figure 23.2):

	True-false answer	Multiple-choice answer		True-false answer	Multiple-choice answer
3.	F	b	25.	T	d
6.	F	c	28.	T	c
9.	T	a	29.	T	c
13.	T	d	34.	F	a
15.	T	a	40.	F	c
18.	T	b	41.	F	d
21.	T	b	44.	F	d
24.	F	a	45.	F	b

Write Your Answers Clearly. When you answer questions on an objective test in college, print your answers clearly so they are easy for the person who scores your answer sheet to read:

A B C D T F

Sometimes when students are uncertain of a correct answer they make letters that are very difficult to read:

Are the first two letters *F*'s or *T*'s? Is the third letter an *a* or a *d*? Is the fourth letter a *B* or a *D*? Avoid making letters that are difficult to read because college professors are likely to score any such responses as incorrect.

Check Your Answers Carefully. Some students answer objective test questions very quickly and turn in their answer sheets without double-checking their answers. This habit often lowers test scores, because one careless error can make the difference between a B and a C grade, or between a C and a D.

However, you should be careful about changing answers once you have written them down. Researchers have found that some people are likely to change correct answers to incorrect answers; this is something you do not want to do. Study your answer sheets when they are returned to you to determine if you change incorrect answers to correct answers or if you are more likely to change correct answers to incorrect answers. Be cautious about changing answers if you discover that you frequently change correct answers to incorrect answers.

Do Not Be Concerned About Other Test-Takers. When you are taking any test, concentrate on what you are doing and try not to be concerned about what other test-takers are doing. If possible, take a seat by yourself and be certain that nobody sits in the seats next to you. You need all the privacy you can get so you can give your full concentration to doing your best. If you cannot avoid sitting next to another student, sit in such a way that it is not possible for your neighbor to see your answers. Some college professors who are very pleasant at all other times become exceedingly disagreeable when they see students sharing answers to test questions. If your neighbor can see your answer sheet, your instructor might incorrectly conclude that this is what you intend.

Also, do not be concerned if some students finish the test before you do. Researchers have studied students' scores on tests in relation to the time they spent working on tests. They have discovered that some students finish quickly because they have mastered the material, while others finish early because they do not know the answers to many questions. They have also discovered that some of the students who finish last are especially cautious when taking tests and earn very high scores, while others who take a long time to finish do very poorly. In other words, it has been established that there is little relationship between test scores and the amount of time spent answering test questions. Therefore, do not assume that students who finish a test before you have done better on it than you will do.

OBJECTIVE TESTS CAN BE DIFFICULT

Students are often pleased to learn that an instructor will give an objective test because they believe that it is easier to earn a high score on an objective test than on an essay test. However, true-false, multiple-choice, and matching questions are not necessarily easier than essay questions. A well-made objective test can be very challenging, especially when it contains many questions based on the kinds of information described in Lesson 11: confusing information, unexpected facts, and the apparently familiar.

A second reason that objective tests can be difficult is that often the questions are written in such a way that every word must be read carefully and interpreted accurately if they are to be answered correctly. The basic purpose of the next four lessons is to give you practice that will help you develop the habit of reading and interpreting objective test questions with great care.

Lesson 24. Double Negatives

It is well known that it is more difficult to interpret statements that contain negatives (such words as *not*) than it is to interpret statements without negatives. This lesson should help you become better at interpreting objective test questions containing negatives.

PRETEST FOR DOUBLE NEGATIVES

Evaluate your ability to interpret statements that contain double negatives by marking the following statements "T" if they are true or "F" if they are false:

_____ 1. Diane is pretty, so it is not unfalse to say she is easy on the eyes.

_____ 2. Bob is smart, so it is not untrue to say he is brainy.

_____ 3. Dr. Thurston is a well-liked professor, so it is not disrespectful to be unattentive in his class.

_____ 4. Mrs. Hosey is allergic to smoke, so it is not discourteous to be a nonsmoker in her presence.

_____ 5. Dick is quite handsome, so it is not untrue to say he is not unpleasant to look at.

_____ 6. Rachel is a very good student, so it would not be inaccurate to say she is not incapable of doing well in school.

INTERPRETING DOUBLE NEGATIVES

You should have had some difficulty in trying to decide which statements in the pretest are true and which are false, because all the statements contain at least two negatives. To interpret such statements accurately, it is necessary to cross out the double negatives and then read the statements for meaning. The following is an explanation of how such statements are read:

> *When there are two negatives, cross out both negatives—the double negative.*
>
> 1. Diane is pretty, so it is ~~not un~~false to say she is easy on the eyes. (*False*—it is true to say she is easy on the eyes.)
> 2. Bob is smart, so it is ~~not un~~true to say he is brainy. (*True.*)

209

When there are three negatives, cross out only the double negative.

3. Dr. Thurston is a well-liked professor, so it is n̶o̶t̶ d̶i̶s̶respectful to be <u>un</u>attentive in his class. (*False*—it is not respectful to be unattentive in a class.)
4. Mrs. Hosey is allergic to smoke, so it is n̶o̶t̶ d̶i̶s̶courteous to be a <u>non</u>smoker in her presence. (*True*—it is courteous not to smoke in her presence.)

When there are four negatives, cross out both double negatives.

5. Dick is quite handsome, so it is n̶o̶t̶ u̶n̶true to say he is n̶o̶t̶ u̶n̶pleasant to look at. (*True*—he is pleasant to look at.)
6. Rachel is a very good student, so it would n̶o̶t̶ be i̶n̶accurate to say she is n̶o̶t̶ i̶n̶capable of doing well in school. (*True*—it is accurate to say she is capable of doing well in school.)

Some college teachers actually use double negatives in test questions, making statements more difficult to read. Unless you can interpret double negatives quickly and easily, you may lose points on test questions that contain them. The problems for this lesson contain two, three, and four negatives, so that in working them out, you can become more skillful at reading statements that contain double negatives. However, you will probably seldom find test questions containing three or four negatives.

A list of examples of the most common double negatives together with their interpretations follows:

Double negative	Interpretation
<u>not un</u>healthy	healthy
<u>not in</u>direct	direct
<u>not im</u>perfect	perfect
<u>not il</u>legal	legal
<u>not ir</u>responsible	responsible
<u>not non</u>toxic	toxic
<u>not dis</u>agreeable	agreeable

Sometimes one element of a double negative is a negative suffix. Notice how statements need to be rephrased when they contain double negatives with a negative suffix:

Suffix double negative	Interpretation
He is <u>not</u> with<u>out</u> hope.	He has hope.
TV is <u>not</u> with<u>out</u> violence.	There is violence on TV.
We are <u>not</u> with<u>out</u> vision.	We have vision.
She is <u>not</u> sight<u>less</u>.	She has sight.
Things are <u>not</u> hope<u>less</u>.	There is hope.
We are <u>not</u> worth<u>less</u>.	We have worth.

**PRACTICE WITH
INTERPRETING
DOUBLE NEGATIVES**

Solve the following practice problems in the way illustrated in this lesson:

1. When there are two negatives in a statement, cross out both negatives—the double negative.
2. When there are three negatives in a statement, cross out only two of them—the double negative.
3. When there are four negatives in a statement, cross out all four—the two double negatives.

Then read a statement and mark "T" if it is true or "F" if it is false.

Class Practice

Double Negatives

_____ 1. A lie is a statement that is not incorrect.

_____ 2. A wealthy man is not without money.

_____ 3. In winter most trees are not leafless.

_____ 4. Most fine crystal drinking glasses are not unbreakable.

_____ 5. Marilyn Monroe was probably not unaware of her beauty.

_____ 6. Stealing is not an unfriendly thing to do.

_____ 7. A climb up Mt. Everest will not be without danger.

_____ 8. Most dogs are not unwilling to learn to play.

_____ 9. A person cannot write if he is not illiterate.

_____ 10. Stealing and cheating are two things that are usually not inexcusable.

_____ 11. The works of great nonliving artists are not irreplaceable if they are destroyed.

_____ 12. A straight line is not an indirect path from one point to another.

_____ 13. The totally mute are not unable to speak.

_____ 14. Wine is not a nonalcoholic beverage.

_____ 15. It is not illegal in this country to be married to three people at the same time.

_____ 16. A camel is not a humpless animal, nor is a human being a hairless animal.

Assignment 1   **Double Negatives**

_____ 1. Sheets that are not imperfect usually cost less than sheets that are defective.

_____ 2. It would not be unwise to count your chickens before they hatch.

_____ 3. Most people do not prefer to eat in restaurants that are not unclean.

_____ 4. It is not dishonest to tell the truth.

_____ 5. A surprise is something that is not unexpected.

_____ 6. Work not undone is work that has not yet been completed.

_____ 7. If one does a heroic deed, it will not bring dishonor to his family.

_____ 8. A comic is a person who should be not without humor.

_____ 9. When children are between the ages of six and eighteen, they not infrequently go to school.

_____10. French fries are infrequently eaten not unsalted.

_____11. One million dollars is not an insubstantial amount of money.

_____12. A penniless man is not without some money in the bank.

_____13. A secret not spoken is a secret not untold.

_____14. It would not be incorrect to say great beauties are not known for their unwomanliness.

_____15. Most people would not disagree with the statement that a good friend is not to be unkindly treated.

_____16. It is not unconfusing to interpret statements containing more than one negative.

Assignment 2   *Double Negatives*

_____ **1.** It is likely that a person who is interested in others is not friendless.

_____ **2.** When walking a high wire, it is best if one is not careless.

_____ **3.** A person who arrives at work five minutes early is not being untimely.

_____ **4.** It is not dishonest to tell the truth.

_____ **5.** A person who is not undivorced can be a person who is also not unmarried.

_____ **6.** It is not displeasing to learn that a friend is not inconsiderate of your feelings.

_____ **7.** It should not be considered unselfish if only one person in your house selects the TV shows.

_____ **8.** A man totally lacking in kindness may still be not without some other worthwhile characteristics.

_____ **9.** A meal with lamb is not meatless, and a meal not without beef is not meatless either.

_____ **10.** One should not distrust those who have shown they are not to be trusted.

_____ **11.** Clothes that are not unshrinkable will come out of a hot wash not undiminished from their original size.

_____ **12.** It would be untrue to say that washing dishes is not a financially unrewarding occupation.

_____ **13.** The fact that a soldier ran away from a battle cannot be taken as evidence that he was not unafraid.

_____ **14.** If we can learn to do what is not impossible, we should have no difficulty learning to do that which cannot be done.

_____ **15.** A cigarette is not smokeless, nor is it harmless.

_____ **16.** It is best that windows not be shadeless if one wishes that a room not be sunless.

Lesson 25. Specific Determiners

Specific determiners are words such as *always, never,* and *certainly*. It is difficult to interpret statements correctly when they contain such words. This lesson should help you become better at interpreting objective test questions that contain specific determiners.

**PRETEST FOR
SPECIFIC DETERMINERS**

Evaluate your ability to interpret statements that contain specific determiners by marking the following statements "T" if they are true or "F" if they are false:

_____ 1. July is always a summer month.

_____ 2. The shortest route is the best route when you are in a hurry.

_____ 3. Everybody eats at least one meal a day.

_____ 4. There are no people who enjoy suffering.

_____ 5. All people say a "dirty" word now and then.

_____ 6. It is never kind to hang a person upside down by the ankles.

Please decide if the preceding statements are true or false before reading the following explanation.

**INTERPRETING
SPECIFIC DETERMINERS**

When statements are partly false, they must be marked "false," and *each* of the six true-false statements of the pretest is partly false:

1. July is not a summer month in the southern hemisphere.
2. The shortest route might be crowded with traffic, or might run through a body of water or under a mountain. Therefore, it might not be the best route to take when you are in a hurry.
3. Many people in the world starve to death from lack of food; others purposely fast for longer than a month.
4. Masochists enjoy suffering.
5. There must be somebody somewhere who never said a "dirty" word—no matter how you define "dirty." Also, if *say* means "to speak," no person mute since birth has said a "dirty" word.
6. We are hung by our ankles at birth—an act of kindness that starts us breathing.

217

The six true-false statements at the beginning of this lesson contain such words as *always, never,* and *best.* Words such as these are specific determiners; and most of the statements that they are found in are false, because few things in the world meet the requirements imposed by *always, never,* or *best.* Following are lists of the common positive and negative specific determiners:

POSITIVE SPECIFIC DETERMINERS	NEGATIVE SPECIFIC DETERMINERS
all	none
every	not one
everybody	nobody
everyone	no one
always	never
all of the time	at no time
invariably	
will certainly	will certainly not
will definitely	will definitely not
will absolutely	will absolutely not
the best	the worst

It is probably false that *all* people like ice cream, but true that *many* or *quite a few* people like ice cream; it is probably false that *no* woman ever had thirty children, but true that *only a few,* or *not many,* women have ever had thirty children.

PRACTICE WITH INTERPRETING SPECIFIC DETERMINERS

Do the practice problems by (1) underlining the specific determiner in a statement, (2) marking "T" if a statement is true or "F" if a statement is false, and (3) changing false statements to make them true. For example:

_F_ The shortest route is ˄ the <u>best</u> route when you are in a hurry.   *usually*

The specific determiner *best* is underlined, the statement is marked "F" because it is false, and the word *usually* has been added to change the false statement to make it true.

Class Practice

Specific Determiners

_____ **1.** No United States citizen would rather live in a country other than the United States.

_____ **2.** College teachers are always college graduates.

_____ **3.** All American children know the alphabet by the time they are ten years old.

_____ **4.** Taking a nap is the best thing to do for a headache.

_____ **5.** People never spend a day's wages on a meal in a restaurant.

_____ **6.** If this is Monday, tomorrow will certainly be Tuesday.

_____ **7.** All people in this country pay taxes.

_____ **8.** A diet of bananas and peanut butter would give a person the worst nutrition possible.

_____ **9.** Growing children will definitely eat more food than will people over the age of seventy.

_____**10.** No bug is capable of killing a grown man.

_____**11.** A week invariably has seven days.

_____**12.** A person who has never been in a large city will absolutely want to visit one soon.

_____**13.** It is always hot in Miami in December.

_____**14.** It is best to be kind whenever possible.

_____**15.** Plastic dishes never break when dropped.

_____**16.** It is always better to swim in a pool that is full of water than to swim in one that is empty.

Assignment 1　　　　　　　*Specific Determiners*

_____ **1.** No man wants to be mistaken for a woman.

_____ **2.** All of Shakespeare's plays are considered to be his masterpieces.

_____ **3.** A month never has fewer than twenty-eight days in it.

_____ **4.** All college students are high school graduates.

_____ **5.** People never watch television for more than sixteen hours a day.

_____ **6.** The decision to drop out of college is the worst decision a person can make.

_____ **7.** No person will live longer than a day without air or oxygen.

_____ **8.** No college library would have a pornographic book on its shelves.

_____ **9.** Our society would fall apart if people did not obey the laws all of the time.

_____ **10.** Stealing is widely considered to be the worst of crimes.

_____ **11.** All human babies weigh less than 50 pounds at birth.

_____ **12.** Mothers are invariably older than the children to whom they give birth.

_____ **13.** Students who study a great deal invariably receive higher grades than students who study little.

_____ **14.** People who do no work receive no money.

_____ **15.** A man who is a college graduate will definitely make more money than a man who is not.

_____ **16.** If this is May, next month will certainly be June.

Assignment 2   *Specific Determiners*

_____ **1.** A jet plane is the best way for most people to travel 3,000 miles in 6 hours.

_____ **2.** If a man receives a $500 gift, he will definitely not return it to the giver.

_____ **3.** No matter how bad your spelling is, you are certainly not the worst speller in the world.

_____ **4.** If you are always kind to people, people will always be kind to you.

_____ **5.** Healthy children invariably live longer than sickly children.

_____ **6.** The best marriage is the marriage that lasts at least twenty-five years.

_____ **7.** *Time* magazine is sold in every state in the United States of America.

_____ **8.** A century will definitely contain one hundred years.

_____ **9.** A minute is never longer than 60 seconds, if it is accurately measured.

_____ **10.** No fully grown man was ever less than 34 inches tall.

_____ **11.** Without exception, people are taller at age eighteen than they were at age six months.

_____ **12.** People who were treated cruelly by their parents will definitely not treat their own children cruelly.

_____ **13.** A person who has a college degree will absolutely not desire to do work that requires no college degree.

_____ **14.** People never get drunk on one bottle of beer.

_____ **15.** Money always talks.

_____ **16.** A statement that contains a specific determiner is always a false statement.

Lesson 26. Best Choices

In answering multiple-choice questions, you may sometimes come across a question for which the best choice for an answer is the best choice not necessarily because it is true, but because it is the best choice *from among the choices offered*. This lesson should help you become more analytical in selecting the best choices for multiple-choice questions.

PRETEST FOR BEST CHOICES

Evaluate your ability to select the best choices for multiple-choice questions by circling the letter that designates the best choice for the correct answer to the questions that follow. (Ignore for now the lines to the right of the questions.)

1. Football, basketball, and soccer are

   a. played best in the rain. ———

   b. the favorite American sports. ———

   c. team sports of the world. ———

   d. three team sports. ———

2. Coffee, tea, and milk are

   a. beverages. ———

   b. stimulants. ———

   c. liquids. ———

   d. refreshing. ———

3. Oranges, lemons, and grapefruit are

   a. citrus. ———

   b. fruits. ———

   c. yellow. ———

   d. true. ———

4. France, Italy, and Germany are

    a. Mediterranean countries. _____

    b. well-known countries. _____

    c. European countries. _____

    d. like the countries. _____

5. Tuna and sardines are

    a. types of fish. _____

    b. flying fish. _____

    c. large fish. _____

    d. salt water fish. _____

6. The bass drum and xylophone are

    a. types of instruments. _____

    b. percussion instruments. _____

    c. melodic instruments. _____

    d. string instruments. _____

7. Whiskey, wine, and beer are

    a. useful. _____

    b. reddish. _____

    c. beverages. _____

    d. alcoholic. _____

8. Paul Newman and Marilyn Monroe are names of

    a. movie stars. _____

    b. people who perform. _____

    c. unknown entities. _____

    d. lovely women. _____

9. Peaches, apricots, and bananas are

   a. some foods.   _____

   b. fruits with pits.   _____

   c. popular fruits.   _____

   d. seen in pictures.   _____

10. Stoves, refrigerators, and vacuum cleaners are

   a. used for cooking.   _____

   b. household appliances.   _____

   c. used in homes.   _____

   d. sold in clothing stores.   _____

Do your best to select the *best* choice for each item before you read the following correct answers: 1, *d*; 2, *a*; 3, *a*; 4, *c*; 5, *d*; 6, *b*; 7, *d*; 8, *a*; 9, *c*; 10, *b*.

SELECTING BEST CHOICES

The best choice for a multiple-choice question is found not by selecting a true answer but through a process of elimination. In this lesson you will use a process of elimination to select best choices. The process of elimination you will practice using is not the only one that may be used when answering multiple-choice questions, but it is a very useful one in many instances.

The problems for this lesson have been written so that (1) one choice is completely false or impossible, considering the other choices; (2) a second choice is partly false; (3) a third choice is more general than the remaining choice; and (4) the remaining choice is the best choice. The problems are solved by using this four-step process of elimination to find the remaining choice that represents the correct answer. The following examples show the correct solutions to the first two problems of the pretest with which this lesson began:

1. Football, basketball, and soccer are

   a. played best in the rain.   _1_

   b. the favorite American sports.   _2_

   c. team sports of the world.   _3_

   d. three team sports.   _X_

Answer *a* is marked "1" because it is the *false or impossible* answer. These sports are not played best in the rain. Answer *b* is marked "2" because it is *partly false*. Football and basketball are favorite American sports, but soccer is not; soccer is not a favorite American sport in the way football and basketball are. Answer *c* is marked "3" because of the two remaining choices it is *more general*. There are many team sports of the world, but this is a list of only three team sports. Answer *d* is marked "X" because it is the *best choice* after this process of elimination.

Now consider Problem 2.

2. Coffee, tea, and milk are

    a. beverages.   X

    b. stimulants.   2

    c. liquids.   3

    d. refreshing.   1

Answer *d* is marked "1" because although it is not false, it is *impossible— or at least unlikely—considering the other choices*. For one thing, all the other answers are nouns, while *refreshing* is an adjective. Apparently the person who wrote this question wants a noun for an answer. Answer *b* is marked "2" because it is *partly false*. Coffee and tea are stimulants, but milk is not. Answer *c* is marked "3" because it is *more general* than the remaining answer. *Liquids* is a more general term than *beverages;* all beverages are liquids, but not all liquids are beverages. Ocean water, motor oil, and liquid bleach are among the many liquids that are not beverages. Answer *a* is marked "X" because it is the *best choice* after this process of elimination.

PRACTICE WITH SELECTING BEST CHOICES

Enter 1, 2, 3, and X on the lines for Problems 3 through 10 at the beginning of this lesson and for the following practice problems. You will have the best results if you do the problems in exactly the way just illustrated. *First,* put a "1" on the line for the *false or impossible* choice. *Second,* put a "2" on the line for the *partly false* choice. *Third,* put a "3" on the line for whichever remaining answer is *more general*. *Fourth,* put an "X" on the line for the remaining and *best choice*.

If you have difficulty, consider what answers were intended by the person who wrote the questions (see Lesson 23). In this case the person who wrote the questions intended to include one false or impossible answer, one partly false answer, and one more general answer, along with the answer that is the best choice.

Assignment 1   **Best Choices**

1. Sofas, chairs, and benches are

   a. pieces of furniture.   _____

   b. furniture for sitting.   _____

   c. cloth-covered furniture.   _____

   d. friendly and amusing.   _____

2. San Francisco, Los Angeles, and New York are

   a. some U.S. coastal cities.   _____

   b. some U.S. cities.   _____

   c. some West Coast cities.   _____

   d. receiving federal money.   _____

3. *Time, Newsweek,* and *Playboy* are

   a. popular periodicals.   _____

   b. unpopular magazines.   _____

   c. publications of all sorts.   _____

   d. some news magazines.   _____

4. Inches, feet, yards, and miles are

   a. units of measure.   _____

   b. measures of distance.   _____

   c. short distances.   _____

   d. good to know about.   _____

5. Lettuce, spinach, and broccoli are

   a. breakfast treats.   _____

   b. some vegetables.   _____

   c. sometimes eaten raw.   _____

   d. green vegetables.   _____

(*continued*)

6. Cake, pie, and ice cream are

    a. sweet types of food.   _____

    b. popular desserts.   _____

    c. made from fruit.   _____

    d. necessary foods.   _____

7. Pennies, nickels, dimes, and quarters are

    a. coins.   _____

    b. silver.   _____

    c. money.   _____

    d. hard.   _____

8. Cars, busses, and trains are

    a. square-wheeled.   _____

    b. three vehicles.   _____

    c. highway vehicles.   _____

    d. the vehicles.   _____

9. Movies, television, and radio are

    a. means of communication.   _____

    b. eighteenth-century inventions.   _____

    c. visual communications.   _____

    d. the communication media.   _____

10. George Washington, Abraham Lincoln, and Benjamin Franklin are

    a. former Presidents.   _____

    b. great citizens.   _____

    c. famous Americans.   _____

    d. from California.   _____

Assignment 2

Best Choices

If you have difficulty solving any of these problems, look up the meanings of the words that you are not sure you know.

1. Doors, windows, and floors are

    a. found in homes. _____

    b. curious objects. _____

    c. house parts. _____

    d. made of glass. _____

2. Toothpaste, mouthwash, and shampoo are

    a. sold in drugstores. _____

    b. for the mouth. _____

    c. some grooming aids. _____

    d. declining in use. _____

3. Cigars, cigarettes, and pipes are

    a. wrapped tobacco. _____

    b. types of smokes. _____

    c. put in the mouth. _____

    d. often eaten. _____

4. The Mississippi and Columbia

    a. are two rivers. _____

    b. is a train route. _____

    c. are two U.S. rivers. _____

    d. both flow south. _____

5. Rattlers, cobras, and pythons are

    a. types of snakes. _____

    b. poisonous snakes. _____

    c. artificial snakes. _____

    d. deadly snakes. _____

(continued)

6. Spanish, Italian, and German are

    a. some Romance languages.   _____

    b. languages from Europe.   _____

    c. classical languages.   _____

    d. languages of the world.   _____

7. Wool, cotton, nylon, and rayon are

    a. uncommon materials.   _____

    b. synthetic materials.   _____

    c. types of materials.   _____

    d. well-known materials.   _____

8. Australia and England are

    a. great world powers.   _____

    b. large countries.   _____

    c. good places to visit.   _____

    d. English-speaking countries.   _____

9. Baptists, Methodists, and Catholics are

    a. religions.   _____

    b. Protestants.   _____

    c. leaderless.   _____

    d. Christians.   _____

10. Volkswagen, Toyota, and Fiat are

    a. foreign automobiles.   _____

    b. internationally known cars.   _____

    c. European-made cars.   _____

    d. large cars.   _____

Lesson 27. Poorly Written Questions

When you have no idea what the correct answer to a test question might be, it is sometimes possible to find the correct answer by understanding the characteristics of poorly written test questions. This lesson should help you become more analytical when you answer questions on objective tests.

**PRETEST FOR
POORLY WRITTEN QUESTIONS**

Evaluate your ability to select the best choices for poorly written test questions by circling the letters designating the best choice for the correct answer to the following questions:

1. Before adding endings that begin with vowels to root words that end in final silent *e,*
   a. always drop the *e.*
   b. never drop the *e.*
   c. usually drop the *e.*
   d. always change *e* to *i.*

2. Examine this: /p/. This represents
   a. graphemic notation.
   b. morphemic code.
   c. the sound of "p."
   d. a homograph.

3. Which of the following is least likely true with regard to Phi Delta Kappa?
   a. It publishes its own magazine regularly.
   b. Its members are unsympathetic and proud.
   c. It is a national professional organization.
   d. Membership in it is by invitation only.

4. Which of the following is least likely true with regard to vitamins?
   a. Some cookbooks give information about them.
   b. They make people beautiful or more handsome.
   c. Not all known vitamins are needed for health.
   d. Grown men have the least need for vitamin D.

5. Two ounces of 90-proof Scotch contains
   a. 100 calories.
   b. 150 calories.
   c. 175 calories.
   d. 225 calories.

6. Consonant blends consist of
   a. one consonant.
   b. two consonants.
   c. three consonants.
   d. two or three consonants.

7. Which of the following cities is located in the state of New York?
   a. Albany
   b. Rome
   c. Naples
   d. All of the above

Select or guess at answers to the questions before you check your answers and read the explanation that follows. The correct answers are: 1, *c*; 2, *c*; 3, *b*; 4, *b*; 5, *b* or *c*; 6, *d*; and 7, *d*.

CHARACTERISTICS OF POORLY WRITTEN QUESTIONS

The questions that you have just answered are examples of poorly written multiple-choice questions. Each question has a fault in the way it is written that experienced test-takers can use to find the correct answer. The different ways in which multiple-choice items may be poorly written will be described later in this section. However, there is some important information you should have before you read the descriptions.

The things you learn and practice in this lesson are designed primarily to help you become more analytical when you answer multiple-choice questions. This information should be used in test-taking situations only as a last resort and when there is no penalty for guessing. Doing the things described here cannot help students who have not studied achieve passing grades on college tests, but it may help average and above-average students achieve slightly higher test scores. Furthermore, the material in this lesson applies only to poorly written test questions, and so to use this information to its full advantage, you must become skillful at determining when questions are and are not poorly written.

Studies of multiple-choice tests given by college professors have revealed that answers are *likely to be incorrect* when

1. they contain *specific determiners,*
2. they contain *unknown words,*
3. they are *insulting statements,*
4. they are silly or *joke answers,* and
5. they are *extreme choices.*

These studies have also found that answers to multiple-choice test items are *likely to be correct* when

6. they are *longer* or more complete, and
7. they read, "all of the above."

The problems for this lesson have been written so you can use these findings to analyze poorly written multiple-choice items and select the best answers. The seven principles just listed could be used to answer the seven multiple-choice items at the beginning of this lesson, as the following description shows:

1. *Specific determiners are likely to be in incorrect answers.* For the first question of the pretest, you should have selected "usually drop the *e*"

as the correct answer, because all the other answers contain a specific determiner (see Lesson 25).

2. *Unknown words are likely to be in incorrect answers.* For the second question you should have selected "the sound of 'p'" as the correct answer, because all the other answers contain words you probably do not know. Correct answers seldom contain words or phrases students could not possibly know.

3. *Insulting statements are likely to be incorrect answers.* In the third question you were asked to select the least likely true, or incorrect, answer. You should have selected the insult: "Its members are unsympathetic and proud." Correct answers are seldom insults.

4. *Jokes are likely to be incorrect answers.* In the fourth question you were asked to select the least likely true, or incorrect, answer. You should have selected the joke or silly answer: "They make people beautiful or more handsome." If taking vitamins would make us better looking, we would probably all take them daily. Jokes and silly answers are seldom correct.

5. *Extreme choices are likely to be incorrect answers.* In the fifth question you had to select from four numbers: 225, the high extreme; 175 and 150, in the middle range; and 100, the low extreme. You should have eliminated the high extreme (225) and the low extreme (100) and made your choice from *either* 175 *or* 150. The completely correct answer is "150 calories." However, for the purposes of the problems in this lesson, if there are extreme choices, any answer that is not an extreme choice should be considered a correct answer. When in doubt about a correct answer, you may eliminate a high extreme and low extreme answer and select from the middle-range answers:

High extreme (probably false)	Middle range (probably right)	Low extreme (probably wrong)
3.5	1.5 or 2.5	0.5
always	usually, sometimes	never
1850	1790 or 1810	1750
beautiful	attractive, good-looking	ugly

6. *Longer or more complete answers are likely to be correct answers.* For the sixth question you should have selected "two or three consonants" as the correct answer because this is the longer, more complete answer. Longer, more complete answers tend to be correct.

7. *"All of the above" is likely to be a correct answer.* For the seventh question you should have selected "all of the above" as the correct answer. There is a Rome and Naples in New York State! "All of the above" tends to be a correct answer when questions are poorly written.

PRACTICE WITH ANALYZING POORLY WRITTEN QUESTIONS

As you do the practice problems, please keep in mind that the primary purpose of these problems is to help you become more analytical when you take objective tests. You should use these techniques only after you have used all the suggestions given in Lesson 23, and only when you believe that you are dealing with poorly written questions.

Do the following practice problems by circling the letters of the correct answers to the questions and writing alongside each question the clue that led you to the correct answer. You might write: "specific determiners," "unknown words," "insult," "joke," "extreme choices," "longer answer," or "all of the above." The first two problems have been done for you to show you how the remaining problems are to be solved.

Class Practice

Poorly Written Questions

1. Today many teachers and other educators
   a. want to be in show business.
   jokes   b. wear wigs and contact lenses.
   c. put wine in their thermos bottles.
   (d.) belong to a professional union.

2. The United States entered the Second World War in the year
   a. 1918.
   extreme choices   (b.) 1937.*
   (c.) 1941.
   d. 1949.

3. Which of the following is frequently used to punctuate items in a series?
   a. the comma
   b. the semicolon
   c. the colon
   d. both the comma and the semicolon

4. Members of one's family or orientation are usually
   a. blood relatives.
   b. affinal relatives.
   c. tertiary relatives.
   d. misogynistic relatives.

5. English words
   a. never have more than one meaning.
   b. always have more than one meaning.
   c. often have more than one meaning.
   d. always have less than one meaning.

6. *Thwart* means about the same as
   a. stop.
   b. icon.
   c. flout.
   d. abut.

7. Which of the following is least likely true with regard to people who get lost while hiking in the mountains?
   a. They suffer greatly if overexposed to the elements.
   b. They are without good maps or a working compass.
   c. They have an intelligence lower than the average.
   d. They may become anxious about being found.

* The correct answer is 1941, but 1937 should also be considered correct for the purposes of this lesson.

© 1979 by Houghton Mifflin Company

8. A woman has an anxiety reaction that causes her to worry constantly about her dog. This worry interrupts her life so that she does not leave home as often as she might. This woman is
a. completely normal.
b. somewhat abnormal.
c. severely ill.
d. a pyromaniac.

9. The Electra-complex and the Oedipus-complex are observed in
a. boys.
b. girls.
c. children.
d. girls in the case of the Electra-complex and boys in the case of the Oedipus-complex.

10. Before you start writing the answers for an essay test, which of the following should you consider?
a. the time allowed to answer questions
b. the point value for each question
c. the questions easiest for you to answer
d. all of the factors listed above

11. The distance around the middle of the earth at the equator is
a. 24,830 miles.
b. 29,760 miles.
c. 19,620 miles.
d. 33,350 miles.

12. A person who suffers from dipsomania should be kept away from all the following except
a. bourbon.
b. water
c. vodka.
d. gin.

Assignment 1

Poorly Written Questions

1. Readability formulas usually take into account
   a. word length.
   b. sentence length.
   c. paragraph length.
   d. word length and sentence length.

2. George Washington was born in the year
   a. 1712.
   b. 1732.
   c. 1742.
   d. 1762.

3. The sound of *sh* is
   a. always spelled *sh*.
   b. sometimes spelled *s*.
   c. never spelled *ch*.
   d. never spelled *ti*.

4. Which of the following is a digraph?
   a. sh
   b. th
   c. ng
   d. all of the above

5. The median is a measure that is equivalent to
   a. the average.
   b. a coefficient.
   c. a histogram.
   d. the skewness.

6. Which of the following is least likely true with regard to readability formulas?
   a. They measure reading difficulty.
   b. They may be used in any book.
   c. They help infants grow strong.
   d. They vary in their results.

7. The median for a set of numbers may be
   a. equal to the average.
   b. less than the average.
   c. greater than the average.
   d. equal to, less than, or greater than the average.

8. Which of the following is least likely true?
   a. Hitler believed in astrology.
   b. Some psychologists study astrology.
   c. It is stupid to study astrology.
   d. Astrology is increasing in popularity.

(*continued*)

9. In the spelling of English words
   a. *y* is often changed to *i* when adding endings that begin with vowels or consonants.
   b. *y* is always changed to *i* before adding endings that begin with vowels.
   c. *y* is never changed to *i* before adding endings if the *y* is preceded by a consonant.
   d. *y* is always changed to *i* when adding endings that begin with consonants.

10. Which of the following is least likely true with regard to vowels and consonants?
    a. Some words can be spelled using no letters.
    b. Every word contains at least one vowel.
    c. More words begin with consonants than vowels.
    d. Some words contain no consonant letters.

Assignment 2

Poorly Written Questions

1. The letters *w* and *y*
   a. never function as vowels.
   b. sometimes function as vowels.
   c. always function as vowels.
   d. always function as consonants.

2. John F. Kennedy was born in the year
   a. 1904.
   b. 1917.
   c. 1942.
   d. 1920.

3. Morphemes may be
   a. free.
   b. bound.
   c. small.
   d. free or bound.

4. An excellent example of a morpheme would be a
   a. grapheme.
   b. prefix.
   c. phoneme.
   d. barbet.

5. Which of the following is least likely true with regard to morphologists?
   a. They are basic and vulgar.
   b. They are students of language.
   c. They study the parts of words.
   d. They often teach in colleges.

6. Which of the following is least likely true with regard to geminates?
   a. You are more susceptible to them in winter.
   b. They appear frequently in the middle of words.
   c. They are a repetition of the same consonant.
   d. In syllabication they are often separated.

7. Which of the following are cities in Europe?
   a. Paris
   b. Rome
   c. Le Mans
   d. all of the above

8. Which of the following is most likely not true with regard to consonant blends?
   a. They may consist of two or more consonants.
   b. They frequently begin with *s, c,* or *b.*
   c. They are good for you to eat as a snack.
   d. They appear at the beginning of many words.

(continued)

9. Which of the following is most likely not true about a nationally syndicated column that gives advice to people?
   a. It is a widely read newspaper column.
   b. It is written by a foolish, old lady.
   c. It gives advice to many people daily.
   d. It receives many letters each week.

10. The length of the Nile River is
   a. 4,000 miles.
   b. 3,100 miles.
   c. 9,690 miles.
   d. 1,422 miles.

Lesson 28. An Approach to Essay Tests

Essay tests are tests for which students give long, written answers to test questions. They are sometimes called *subjective tests* because they are graded on the basis of the judgments, opinions, and preferences of the person who reads them. When you write answers to an essay test, one instructor might think your answers are worth a B, while another might think they are worth a C. In other words, since your grades on essay tests are subjectively determined, essay tests are sometimes called subjective tests.

TYPES OF ESSAY TESTS

There are several different ways in which essay tests can be administered. Usually, students do not see the test questions until they arrive at the test session and thus must answer the questions from memory. However, in the *open-book* test, students are allowed to refer to their textbooks while writing the answers to test questions. When *take-home* tests are given, students take the test questions "home," answer them, and return the answers to their professors. Another variation is the *take-home, open-book* test. In this kind of test, students are given test questions to study at home, but they answer the questions in class either with their books open or from memory.

It might seem that open-book, take-home, and take-home, open-book tests are easy tests. This is usually not the case, though. Questions on such tests are almost always more difficult than the questions that are presented for the first time in class and answered by students from memory.

**HOW TO PLAN
TEST-TAKING TIME**

One of the problems in doing well on essay tests is that a great deal must be written in a short amount of time. Therefore, when you take an essay test, you need to consider four things in order to make the best use of the available time:

1. *How much time is there for taking the test?* If an essay test is given during a 50-minute class hour, you may have only about 40 minutes of actual test-taking time. Under this condition time becomes of prime importance, but even in a two- or three-hour final examination session, time limitations must be considered carefully.
2. *How many questions must be answered?* Often you are *not* expected to answer every question on an essay test. Typically, an instructor will write five questions and ask students to answer three of them. If students answer all five questions, professors usually grade only the first three answers. If you answer more questions than you are asked to answer, (1) you will probably not receive credit for all your answers, (2) you will waste your time answering questions that will not be graded, and (3) your answers might not represent your best effort because you wasted

time. Therefore, when taking an essay test, it is very important to determine exactly how many questions need to be answered.

3. *What are the point values of questions?* All of the questions on essay tests do not always have the same point values. For example, the answers to some questions may have a value of 10 points, while the answers to others have a value of 30 points. The following example illustrates how a student used the point value of test items to plan test-taking time:

> An instructor gave an essay test that consisted of eight questions. The directions were: "Answer any two of the first five questions and any one of the last three questions. The first five questions have a value of 25 points each and the last three questions have a value of 50 points each." The student was taking the test during a 50-minute class session, and had approximately 40 minutes to answer the questions. She decided to spend about 20 minutes answering the question worth 50 points and about 10 minutes answering each of the questions worth 25 points.

Always find out the exact point value of essay questions and use this information to help you plan your test-taking time. You want to give most of your attention to the questions that are worth the most points.

4. *Which question can be answered most quickly?* The student in the previous example discovered there was a 25-point question that she could answer in 5 minutes. She answered that question first, spent 10 minutes answering the other 25-point question, and then had 25 minutes to answer the 50-point question and proofread her answers.

HOW TO WRITE ESSAY ANSWERS

Professors who give essay tests know that students write answers under pressure and, therefore, do not have time to turn out their best written work. There is seldom time during an essay test to rewrite what you wrote as you would do when writing papers outside of class. However, you should keep in mind two basic objectives when you write answers to essay questions. *First,* it is your task to convince your professors that you know course content. *Second,* since professors have many essay tests to read, you should do everything you can to make it easy for them to read and understand your answers. These objectives are achieved by doing the things you probably have learned in your writing courses—namely, organizing your answer, writing an introductory statement that summarizes your answer, providing good details to back up your introductory statement, and proofreading what you have written.

Organize Your Answer Before You Write. Before you start to write your answer, you should have a good idea of exactly how you will organize it. You may make outlines of your answers before writing them, but often this is not necessary. Lesson 30 describes ways to decide on the organization of answers to essay questions.

Make Your Introductory Statement a Summary of Your Answer. An introduction to an essay question answer should be a summary of the answer.

Avoid the mistake commonly made by many students—beginning an essay question answer with a long-winded or flowery introduction that contributes little or nothing to the informational content of the answer. Instead, make your opening statement a clear summary of your basic answer to the question and use the rest of your essay to expand on your introductory statement. Two sample essay questions and the introductory statements that might be used to answer them are as follows:

QUESTION 1

Discuss three ways property may be acquired.

ESSAY INTRODUCTION 1

We studied three ways in which property may be acquired: (1) inheritance, (2) legacy, and (3) accession.

QUESTION 2

Describe four basic types of family relationships.

ESSAY INTRODUCTION 2

The four basic types of family relationships are the nuclear family, extended family, monogamous family, and polygamous family.

A clear, concise introduction helps you write a good answer to a question and helps your teachers read and understand your answer.

Always Include Details and Examples in Your Answers. The best way to demonstrate that you understand something is to include supporting details and examples. You should do this every time you write an answer for an essay question, even if the answer is a short one. For example:

QUESTION

Explain sex-typing.

ANSWER WITH NO DETAILS OR EXAMPLES

Sex-typing occurs when parents encourage behaviors in a child that are appropriate to the child's sex. It is very important in the socialization of children and should not be overlooked.

ANSWER WITH DETAILS AND EXAMPLES

> *Sex-typing is observed when parents encourage behaviors in children that they think are appropriate for their sexes and discourage behaviors that they think are not appropriate for their sexes. For example, some parents might encourage boys to play roughly but discourage this in girls. Boys might be taught to play baseball, while girls are encouraged to play "house."*

Examples make it evident to the reader that the person who wrote the second short essay completely understands sex-typing. Use details and examples in your essay answers so it is clear to your teachers that you completely understand course content.

Proofread Your Answers. Although you are not expected to turn in your best writing when you answer essay questions under time limitations, you should always plan for time at the end of a session in which to proofread your answers. Check for misspelled words, awkward phrasing, and so on.

Outline Answers You Do Not Have Time to Write Completely. If you should ever have too little time to write a complete answer for a question, you should write an outline of the answer you would have written if you had had the time to do so. You might show your outline answer to your professor and ask if you can have additional time to write the answer. *Do not leave a question unanswered or write an incomplete answer to a question simply because you are pressed for time.* If no answer is written, your professor will assume you did not know the answer. If you write a very brief, incomplete answer, your instructor will conclude that you wrote the best answer you could write and will grade it accordingly. Therefore, outline answers you cannot finish within the time limit and request additional time to complete your answers in written form.

Lessons 29 and 30 will help you understand two problems in answering essay test questions correctly.

Lesson 29. Direction Words

One major problem in answering essay questions is to understand the meanings of *direction words*. Examples of direction words are underlined in the following sample essay questions:

> Define *frustration*.
> Compare the nuclear family, extended family, and primary relatives.
> Discuss schizophrenia.

It is difficult to state exactly what a particular direction word might mean every time it appears in essay test questions, but the meanings of direction words in essay questions are very much the same as their meanings in everyday life.

**TEN COMMONLY USED
DIRECTION WORDS**

It would be impossible or impractical to discuss all of the many different direction words. But following are explanations of the meanings of the ten commonly used direction words that are used in the problems for this lesson.

Discuss. *Discuss* is the most general of all the direction words. When you discuss something, you examine it in as much detail as you can within the time limits provided. Almost any topic can be discussed: a movie you saw, the price of automobiles, people you know, and so on.

> Discuss the problems involved in identifying derivatives that contain an English root word.
> Discuss the effects of television advertising on the buying habits of the American people.

Explain. *Explain* has more than one meaning, but only one will be considered here: when you explain something, you give reasons. When you explain to a friend why you cannot go out one night or when you explain to an employer why you were absent from work, you give reasons.

> Explain the importance of being familiar with the information that appears in your college catalog.
> Explain why one should carry five different types of automobile insurance.

247

Relate. *Relate* also has more than one meaning, but only one is discussed here: *relate* means to show how two things are connected, or related, to each other. For example:

> Relate population growth to a reduction in the quality of life on earth.
>
> Relate television advertising to poor dietary habits in this country.

Summarize. *Summarize* means to give the main points about something in brief form. The word *summarize,* though, is not always a clue to a short answer. For example:

> Summarize the major changes in the power of the Presidency of the United States, beginning with George Washington and continuing up to the present time.

Entire books have been written on this theme, so *summarize* does not necessarily indicate that a short answer is wanted.

Enumerate and List. *Enumerate* and *list* have similar meanings: give statements one by one so the major points stand out clearly.

> Enumerate the direction words used in essay test questions, and give a brief definition of each.
>
> List the things to consider when taking an essay test.

When the word *enumerate* or *list* appears in an essay question, it is a specific request for you to make the major points stand out clearly. This may be done by numbering your major points or by using a separate paragraph for each major point and underlining key words. It is always a good idea to give readers of your essays all the help you can so they will find your major points.

Compare. The meaning of *compare* is often misinterpreted. *Compare* means to show how two things are alike and how they are different. If you were to compare going to college and going to high school, you would show both differences and similarities.

> Compare communism and capitalism.
>
> Compare regressive, progressive, and proportional taxes.

If your answer to the first question described only the similarities between communism and capitalism, it would be an incomplete answer and would not receive full credit.

Contrast. When you *contrast* two things, you emphasize how they are different. When making a contrast, you might mention some similarities, but you should emphasize differences.

Contrast the characteristics of students with good study habits to those of students with poor study habits.
Contrast the Baroque style of music to that of the eighteenth-century classicists.

Criticize. *Criticize,* like *contrast,* is a direction word that is often misinterpreted. We are so accustomed to thinking of critical remarks as unfavorable remarks that when we are asked to criticize something, we often give only negative or unfavorable comments. However, you know that when you read the critique of a movie, the movie critic may have only good things to say, only bad things to say, or both good and bad things to say. When you criticize something, give the good points and the bad points, the strengths and the weaknesses.

Criticize this statement: "Sales taxes are regressive and, therefore, should be abolished."
Criticize Sheldon's and Eysenck's theories of personality.

A criticism is not usually very effective when it is based solely on the feelings or opinions of the critic. When you criticize something, try to bring in authorities to support the points of view you express. The writers of books you read and the instructors of your courses are among the authorities you might wish to consider.

Describe. When you *describe* something, the person reading your description can visualize the thing or process you describe. If you do a good job describing a trip you took, people who read your description will be able to picture the places you visited and the people you met. When answering essay questions, you may be asked to describe a procedure so it can be visualized.

Describe an efficient method to use when studying for a college test.
Describe the characteristics of a textbook that has been well underlined or highlighted.

Define. When you *define* a word or term, you give a statement of its meaning and include an example, if possible.

Define *frustration.*

To answer this question, you would state the meaning of *frustration* and give an example.

PRACTICE WITH INTERPRETING DIRECTION WORDS

The practice problems are examples of essay test questions in which direction words are printed in italic type. You are to rewrite the questions so the direction word is eliminated, but the question is preserved. For example:

Define *frustration.*

For this essay question, you would write:

Give the meaning of frustration.

The following list contains direction words together with phrases that you may use to help you solve the problems:

1. *Discuss* means "give as much information as you can."
2. *Explain* means "give reasons."
3. *Relate* means "show how _____ and _____ are connected or related."
4. *Summarize* means "briefly tell."
5. *Enumerate* and *list* mean "make the major points stand out clearly."
6. *Compare* means "show how _____ and _____ are alike and different."
7. *Contrast* means "show how _____ and _____ are different."
8. *Criticize* means "show the good points and bad points, the strengths and weaknesses."
9. *Describe* means "make it possible to visualize."
10. *Define* means "give the meaning."

Class Practice

Direction Words

1. <u>Discuss</u> the various kinds of college degrees.

   _____

   _____

   _____

   _____

2. <u>Explain</u> the importance of considering sex, religious and political affiliations, and educational background of an audience when preparing a serious speech.

   _____

   _____

   _____

   _____

3. Tell how trademarks and trade names are <u>related</u>.

   _____

   _____

_____

_____

4. <u>Summarize</u> how direct-mail advertising, direct-response advertising, and mail-order advertising might be used to sell books or records.

_____

_____

_____

_____

5. <u>Enumerate</u> the reasons for giving tests.

_____

_____

_____

_____

6. <u>Compare</u> description, narration, and exposition.

_____

_____

_____

_____

7. <u>Contrast</u> the uses of (1) *to, too,* and *two,* and (2) *they're, their,* and *there.*

_____

_____

_____

_____

8. <u>Criticize</u> this statement: ''McDonald's could increase hamburger sales by using all the steps in the selling process.''

_____

_____

_____

_____

9. <u>Describe</u> how the steps in the selling process might be used by a company that sells low-cost vacations.

_____

_____

_____

_____

10. <u>Define</u> *ambivalent attitude*.

_____

_____

_____

_____

Assignment 1   *Direction Words*

1. <u>Discuss</u> real property and personal property.

   _____

   _____

   _____

   _____

2. <u>Explain</u> the importance of each step in the SOAR study formula.

   _____

   _____

   _____

   _____

3. <u>Relate</u> primary relatives to nuclear family.

   _____

   _____

   _____

   _____

4. <u>Summarize</u> the things to consider when taking objective tests.

   _____

   _____

   _____

   _____

5. <u>Enumerate</u> the various kinds of automobile insurance.

   _____

   _____

   _____

   _____

(continued)

6. <u>Compare</u> schizophrenia and the manic-depressive condition.

_____

_____

_____

_____

7. <u>Contrast</u> the halo effect and stereotypes.

_____

_____

_____

_____

8. <u>Criticize</u> this statement: "Objective tests are superior to subjective tests."

_____

_____

_____

_____

9. <u>Describe</u> the differences among primary, secondary, and tertiary relatives.

_____

_____

_____

_____

10. <u>Define</u> _polygamy_.

_____

_____

_____

_____

Assignment 2

Direction Words

1. <u>Discuss</u> the importance of having good organizational skills for whatever line of work you intend to pursue.

   _____

   _____

   _____

   _____

2. <u>Explain</u> why you are attending college.

   _____

   _____

   _____

   _____

3. <u>Relate</u> what you are studying in college to what you expect to do after you earn a college degree.

   _____

   _____

   _____

   _____

4. Identify four people and <u>summarize</u> the ways in which each has had an important influence on you.

   _____

   _____

   _____

   _____

5. <u>List</u> the characteristics you most admire in your close friends.

   _____

   _____

   _____

   _____

(continued)

6. <u>Compare</u> a class you enjoy attending and one you do not like to attend.

_____

_____

_____

_____

7. <u>Contrast</u> the person you are to the person you intend to become.

_____

_____

_____

_____

8. <u>Criticize</u> this statement: "People achieve success in life when they attain the worthwhile goals they have set for themselves."

_____

_____

_____

_____

9. <u>Describe</u> your appearance, dwelling place, employment, financial situation, and companions as they will be twenty years from today.

_____

_____

_____

_____

10. <u>Define</u> this phrase: "my ideal marriage partner."

_____

_____

_____

_____

Lesson 30. Organizing Essay Answers

Once you understand how to interpret direction words in essay questions (see Lesson 29), a second major problem in answering essay questions is to write well-organized answers. If your answers are well organized, (1) you will be more likely to write complete answers and (2) it will be easy for your professors to read and understand your answers.

QUESTIONS WITH MORE THAN ONE PART

Many times a single essay question will require you to do more than one thing, and your answers to such questions will not be complete unless you do all the things requested by such questions. Following are examples of essay questions requiring students to do two different things:

QUESTION 1

Identify the steps in the selling process and show how a specific business might use all five of the steps to sell a product or service.

To answer this question, the test-taker would first need to identify the five steps in the selling process: (1) find a buyer, (2) meet the buyer under favorable conditions, (3) present the product in an attractive or convincing way, (4) stimulate the customer's desire to buy, and (5) close the sale. Then the test-taker would need to show how a specific business might use all the steps. If the example of a moving company were selected, advertising might be shown to be a means of finding a buyer. If the moving company is in a large city, a favorable condition for business might be during the first part of any month because most apartment leases end at the beginning of the month. All the steps in the selling process would need to be similarly illustrated.

QUESTION 2

Define *nuclear family, extended family, primary relatives,* and *secondary relatives.* Then show how the types of relatives and types of families are related to each other.

To answer this question, the test-taker would first need to define the four terms, giving their meanings along with appropriate illustrations. Next, the test-taker would need to show that the nuclear family can be a *family of orientation* or a *family of procreation.* The relationship between the two types of nuclear families and primary relatives would need to be given. Finally, the test-taker would need to explain how the extended family might be composed of primary and secondary relatives. An answer to this question would be incomplete if it did not do all these things.

When you write answers to essay test questions, it is very important that you make certain you have done all the things the questions request you to do. If you do not, you will not receive full credit for your answers.

QUESTIONS THAT GIVE OUTLINES FOR ANSWERS

Often the outlines for answers to essay questions are given in the questions. Following are two essay test questions and the outlines stated in them:

QUESTION 1

Describe what happens at each step of the SOAR study formula: survey before you read, organize what you read, anticipate test questions, and recite and review.

A test-taker may answer this question using the outline that is given in it:

SOAR
   I. Survey before you read.
   II. Organize what you read.
   III. Anticipate test questions.
   IV. Recite and review.

QUESTION 2

Relate the primary relatives (mother, father, brothers, sisters, spouse, sons, and daughters) to the nuclear family (family of orientation and family of procreation).

The test-taker may answer this question using the outline that is given in it:

PRIMARY RELATIVES AND NUCLEAR FAMILY
   I. Primary relatives
      A. Mother
      B. Father
      C. Sisters
      D. Brothers
      E. Spouse
      F. Sons
      G. Daughters
   II. Nuclear family
      A. Family of orientation
      B. Family of procreation

It is a great aid to the test-taker when instructors include outlines in essay test questions.

QUESTIONS THAT DO NOT GIVE OUTLINES FOR ANSWERS

The test questions that were used as examples in the preceding discussion could have been written so the outlines for their answers had to be recalled by the test-takers. Here is how the questions might have been written with the outlines removed:

QUESTION 1

Describe the steps of the SOAR study formula.

QUESTION 2

Relate primary relatives to the nuclear family.

Questions of this type can be answered correctly only by students who have studied and learned the organization of ideas. In this lesson you will practice finding the outlines for essay questions when the outlines are *not* stated in essay questions.

PRACTICE WITH OUTLINING ESSAY ANSWERS

The practice problems consist of a sample essay test question followed by the number of the page in this book on which the answer to the question may be found. Following is a sample problem and its solution; the solution was found by referring to the passage entitled "Sheldon's Somatotypes" on page 193.

> Describe the physical and personality characteristics of Sheldon's somatotypes. (page 193)
>
> I. Endomorphs
>
> II. Ectomorphs
>
> III. Mesomorphs

Please note that you are not to write the answer to a question; you are only to give the outline you would use to write the answer. As further samples, the solutions to the first two practice problems have been started for you.

If desired, you may also practice writing answers to essay questions by using some of the questions in this lesson or in Lesson 29. If you do this, you may evaluate the essay answers you write by determining if your answers meet the following criteria:

1. They are the kinds of answers required by the questions. (For example, when asked to *contrast* two things, you show how they are alike *and* different.)
2. They begin with introductions that summarize the points that follow.
3. They are well organized.
4. They include good details and examples.

These are the characteristics of well-written answers to essay test questions.

Class Practice

Essay Outlines

1. Explain the general rules to follow when taking a test. (pages 161–162)

I. *Read and follow directions*

II. *Easy questions are answered first*

III.

IV.

2. Describe how one should go about preparing for a test. (page 162)

I. *Use all the study skills you know*

3. Define *polygamy*. (page 167)

4. Enumerate the various kinds of automobile insurance. (pages 57–58)

© 1979 by Houghton Mifflin Company

5. Criticize this statement: "Objective tests are superior to essay tests."
(page 163)

_____

_____

_____

_____

_____

_____

6. Explain the importance of each factor used to determine people's credit
ratings. (pages 174–175)

_____

_____

_____

_____

_____

_____

Assignment 1

Essay Outlines

1. Explain the importance of each of the characteristics of people that should be considered when preparing a serious speech. (page 162)

   I. Sex

   _____

   _____

   _____

2. Enumerate the reasons for giving tests. (page 164)

   _____

   _____

   _____

   _____

   _____

3. Summarize the sources of consumer credit. (pages 175–177)

   _____

   _____

   _____

   _____

4. What are the symptoms of schizophrenia? (page 166)

   _____

   _____

   _____

   _____

(*continued*)

5. Discuss the different types of family relationships. (pages 166–167)

_____

_____

_____

_____

6. Tell what you know about the different kinds of relatives. (page 173)

_____

_____

_____

_____

_____

Assignment 2

Essay Outlines

1. What considerations determined the site of Washington, D.C.? (page 179)

   _____

   _____

   _____

2. Discuss the major issues associated with the dating system in our country. (pages 182–187)

   _____

   _____

   _____

   _____

   _____

   _____

3. Summarize the ways in which property might be acquired. (page 57)

   _____

   _____

   _____

   _____

4. Contrast the concerns of the behavioral scientists. (page 61)

   _____

   _____

   _____

   _____

   _____

   _____

(continued)

5. Identify the various states of the manic-depressive psychotic condition.
   (page 166)

   I. _____

       A. _____

       B. _____

   II. _____

6. Show how primary relatives and the nuclear family are related. (pages
   166 and 173)

   I. Family of orientation _____

       A. Mother _____

   _____

   _____

   _____

   _____

   _____

   _____

   _____

   _____

Some Final Words

In your study of this book you have learned skills you can use to study for college courses and to be well organized on almost any job you might have. If you have already applied these skills in courses you are taking, you should recognize their value.

**DEVELOPING YOUR OWN
STUDY STYLE**

Good study and test-taking skills are not developed in a few weeks; they are refined over years of practice. When you have difficulty studying or when you want to make even better use of your study time, you should return to this book and refresh your memory about good study procedures. Also, there are probably some skills covered in this book that you have not yet had an opportunity to use in the courses you are currently taking. You should review what is said about those skills at the times you need to use them. For example, if you have not yet taken an essay test, you should review what is said in this book about essay tests when an instructor of yours schedules such a test.

When you use the study skills you have learned, you will find yourself adapting them in various ways to suit your special needs and learning style. This is as it should be. When you adapt the suggestions in this book so they are more useful to you when you study, you will know you are becoming a talented student.

**THE VALUE OF
YOUR EDUCATION**

As students, we usually are all too aware of the sacrifices we make for our college educations. The cost of tuition is high, we must sometimes take courses we would rather not take, and we must spend much of our time studying rather than doing other things we might want to do.

However, we often fail to consider that others have given greatly so we might attend college. Tuition, high though it is, often pays for less than one-half of a college education! The rest is paid through taxes and contributions made by people we will never meet. The teachers, staff, buildings, grounds, and equipment needed for colleges are provided for us, in large part, by people who do not know us but who want us to live fuller lives. Some of these people want us to have the benefits of the education they received in college; others want us to have the benefits of the college education they missed.

The proportion of students attending college is far greater in this country than in any other country because of the generosity of our citizens who support colleges and entrust our educations to them. In return for this trust placed in them, colleges offer instruction in study skills, writing, and mathematics to help ensure that students will earn their degree. Most colleges also provide counselors and advisers as well as other student services to increase the likelihood that the college experience is successful. But we are not forced to use the things we are taught, nor to use the other services that are provided for us—we must decide for ourselves if we will benefit from the help we are offered.

When we take advantage of the opportunities we are given, we help ourselves and we also repay the efforts of those who have tried to help us. You will never meet most of the people who contributed financial support to your education, but during your college years you will meet many of the people on your campus who have devoted their lives to college education. You will benefit from getting to know some of these people. Your college experience will be richer if you find faculty and staff members at your school who will be your friends and take a special interest in you. You will help yourself, and, in turn, you will reward them by giving them a chance to know you and to learn from you.

People you know, and many people you do not know, give their talent, energy, and money so you will remember college as a time of growth, learning, and happiness. You repay them when you decide you will become an educated person. If you have made this decision, you have enriched yourself and rewarded all those who want for you the very best in life.

© 1979 by Houghton Mifflin Company

Glossary of College Words

Words within the definitions that are printed in *italics* are defined in this glossary.

Alumni. All the graduates of a school. If all the graduates are women, the correct term is alumn*ae*.

Assistant professor. A rank for a college teacher that is lower than the rank of *associate professor* but higher than the rank of *instructor*.

Associate degrees. *Degrees* offered by two-year colleges, usually the A.A. (Associate of Arts), A.S. (Associate of Science), or A.A.S. (Associate of Applied Science).

Associate professor. A rank for a college teacher that is lower than the rank of *professor* but higher than the rank of *assistant professor*.

Audit. To have official permission to attend a course, but not to receive *credit* for the course.

Bachelor's degrees. *Degrees* offered by four-year colleges, usually the B.A. (Bachelor of Arts) or B.S. (Bachelor of Science).

Bluebooks. Booklets containing lined paper, in which students write essays or answers to essay test questions.

Bursar. The title of a person at a college who is responsible for money transactions; a treasurer.

Class card. A card for a college class (usually an IBM card) given to students who are officially enrolled in the class.

Course number. A number that designates a particular course offered by a college. For example, EN-101 might designate a course offered by an English department.

Credits. Units given for completion of any study that applies toward a college *degree*.

Curriculum. The courses required to earn a particular *degree*.

Deans. Members of the administration of a college who are in charge of specified aspects of the school's activities, such as dean of faculty, dean of instruction, and dean of students.

Degrees. Ranks given to students who have successfully completed specified courses of study, usually *associate degrees, bachelor's degrees, master's degrees,* or *doctoral degrees.*

Department. Within a college, a unit that offers courses in a specific subject or a specific group of subjects. For example, a history department might offer only courses in history; a social sciences department may offer courses in psychology, sociology, anthropology, and other subjects.

Division. In some colleges, *departments* are organized under larger groups called divisions. For example, the social sciences division of a college may include a psychology department, sociology department, anthropology department, and other departments.

Doctoral degrees. The highest *degrees* offered by colleges and universities. Many college teachers earn a Ph.D. (Doctor of Philosophy) or Ed.D. (Doctor of Education).

Elective. A course that students may take but that they are not required to take to earn a *degree*.

Freshmen. Students in their first *undergraduate* year of study at a college or university.

Grade point average. A number that ranges from 0.00 to 4.00 and indicates students' average course grades.

Grade point values. Values given to letter grades so that *grade point averages* may be computed. The following values are used by many colleges: A, 4.00; B, 3.00; C, 2.00; D, 1.00; and F, 0.00.

Hours. Units, usually less or more than an actual hour long, that designate the time spent in classroom, laboratory, or conference for courses.

Incomplete (INC). A grade given at many colleges when students are doing passing work but have not completed all course requirements. Usually an INC grade is changed to F or some other grade if incomplete work is not completed within a specified time.

Instructor. A title for college teachers who have the rank lower than *assistant professor*.

Juniors. Students in their third *undergraduate* year of study at a college or university.

Lecturer. A title sometimes applied to college teachers who do not have the rank or *tenure* of *professors* or *instructors*.

Letter grades. Grades such as B+, C, and D− that designate the quality of work students do. Letter grades have the following meanings at many colleges: A, excellent; B, good; C, satisfactory; D, passing; and F, failing.

Lower division. The first two years of college study; the *freshman* and *sophomore* years.

Master's degrees. *Degrees* that rank higher than *bachelor's degrees* but lower than *doctoral degrees,* usually the M.A. (Master of Arts) or M.S. (Master of Science).

Matriculation. A classification for individuals who are currently accepted by colleges or universities to study for *degrees*.

Number grades. Grades such as 91, 85, and 68 that designate the quality of work students do. Many colleges agree on the following correspondences between number grades and *letter grades:* A, 90–100; B, 80–89; C, 70–79; D, 60–69; and F, 0–59.

Pass/fail. A grading system that permits students to receive only passing or failing grades. *Letter grades* such as A, B, and C are not given when courses are taken on a pass/fail basis.

Prerequisite. A requirement that must be completed before a course may be taken. For example, the prerequisite for an intermediate algebra course may be a course in elementary algebra.

Probation. A classification into which students are put while they attempt to raise low *grade point averages* or to remove other academic deficiencies.

Professor. The highest rank for college teachers, also sometimes called full professor to distinguish from *associate professor* and *assistant professor*.

Quarter system. A system that divides a school year into three parts, usually a fall, winter, and spring *term* of ten weeks each.

Registrar. The title of a person at a college who is responsible for registering students in courses and for maintaining their academic records on *transcripts*.

Section number. A number used when there are two or more sections (classes) for the same course to designate where, when, and by whom a specific section for a course is taught.

Semester system. A system that divides a school year into two parts, usually a fall and spring *term* of fifteen to sixteen weeks each.

Seminar. A small group of students who meet under the supervision of a teacher to discuss reading, research, writing, or other work they have done.

Seniors. Students in their fourth *undergraduate* year of study at a college or university.

Sophomores. Students in their second *undergraduate* year of study at a college or university.

Summer session. A period in the summer during which students may take courses for academic *credit* but which is not usually considered a *semester* or *quarter* for the purposes of a school's business.

Suspension. A classification into which students are put that prevents them from attending school for a specified period of time.

Tenure. A status that college teachers may achieve which assures them they will hold their teaching positions permanently.

Term. A period of study in a college. A term may be a *semester,* a *quarter,* or a *summer session.*

Transcripts. Official records of courses taken, grades received, and *grade point averages.*

Undergraduates. College students who have not yet earned *bachelor's degrees.*

Upper division. The third and fourth years of study in a four-year college; the *junior* and *senior* years.

Withdrawal (W). A grade given at many colleges so that students may drop courses when they have good reasons for doing so. Usually W grades do not lower *grade point averages* when they are requested within specified time limits or when students are doing passing work at the time of withdrawal.

Index

STUDY SCHEDULE*

	MON	TUE	WED	THU	FRI	SAT	SUN
8–9							
9–10							
10–11							
11–12							
12–1							
1–2							
2–3							
3–4							
4–5							
5–6							
6–7							
7–8							
8–9							
9–10							
10–11							

* Use pencil so you can make changes.

STUDY SCHEDULE*

	MON	TUE	WED	THU	FRI	SAT	SUN
8–9							
9–10							
10–11							
11–12							
12–1							
1–2							
2–3							
3–4							
4–5							
5–6							
6–7							
7–8							
8–9							
9–10							
10–11							

* Use pencil so you can make changes.

STUDY SCHEDULE*

	MON	TUE	WED	THU	FRI	SAT	SUN
8–9							
9–10							
10–11							
11–12							
12–1							
1–2							
2–3							
3–4							
4–5							
5–6							
6–7							
7–8							
8–9							
9–10							
10–11							

* Use pencil so you can make changes.

STUDY SCHEDULE*

	MON	TUE	WED	THU	FRI	SAT	SUN
8–9							
9–10							
10–11							
11–12							
12–1							
1–2							
2–3							
3–4							
4–5							
5–6							
6–7							
7–8							
8–9							
9–10							
10–11							

* Use pencil so you can make changes.

STUDY SCHEDULE*

	MON	TUE	WED	THU	FRI	SAT	SUN
8–9							
9–10							
10–11							
11–12							
12–1							
1–2							
2–3							
3–4							
4–5							
5–6							
6–7							
7–8							
8–9							
9–10							
10–11							

* Use pencil so you can make changes.

STUDY SCHEDULE*

	MON	TUE	WED	THU	FRI	SAT	SUN
8–9							
9–10							
10–11							
11–12							
12–1							
1–2							
2–3							
3–4							
4–5							
5–6							
6–7							
7–8							
8–9							
9–10							
10–11							

* Use pencil so you can make changes.

STUDY SCHEDULE*

	MON	TUE	WED	THU	FRI	SAT	SUN
8–9							
9–10							
10–11							
11–12							
12–1							
1–2							
2–3							
3–4							
4–5							
5–6							
6–7							
7–8							
8–9							
9–10							
10–11							

* Use pencil so you can make changes.

STUDY SCHEDULE*

	MON	TUE	WED	THU	FRI	SAT	SUN
8–9							
9–10							
10–11							
11–12							
12–1							
1–2							
2–3							
3–4							
4–5							
5–6							
6–7							
7–8							
8–9							
9–10							
10–11							

* Use pencil so you can make changes.

ABCDEFGHIJ–SM–798

© 1979 by Houghton Mifflin Company